Arrest Preschoolers or Teach Them Leadership

Arrest Preschoolers or Teach Them Leadership

A Preschool Teacher's Week-by-Week
Workbook for Implementing
Cultural Leadership in the Classroom

C. Jackson Howard PhD

Ancestor Anderson Publishing LLC

Text copyright © 2018 C. Jackson Howard, Design and concept copyright © 2018 Ancestor Anderson Publishing LLC and its licensors. All rights reserved. Any unauthorized duplicate in whole or in part or dissemination of this edition by any means (including but not limited to photocopying, electronic devices, digital versions, and the Internet) will be prosecuted to the fullest extent of the law

Published in the United States by:
Ancestor Anderson Publishing LLC

ISBN: 978-0-9845303-6-6
Library of Congress Control Number:

Printed in the United States

To all the future cultural leaders, and to all the teachers that will support their leadership efforts.

CONTENTS

1		Introduction
9	Chapter 1:	Why Do We Need A Cultural Leadership Workbook
13	Chapter 2:	What's In The Name SCHOLAR? Our Greatest Product
21	Chapter 3:	Why Teach Preschoolers Leadership?
27	Chapter 4:	360 Whole Child *ism*
31	Chapter 5:	Cultural Teaching And The Academic Relationship
35	Chapter 6:	Exploring The Culture Of The Whole Child
39	Chapter 7:	The System: Domains and Competencies Of Cultural Leadership
43	Chapter 8:	Cultural Leadership Competencies
49	Chapter 9:	Wellness, Leadership and Education
53	Chapter 10:	The Depth of Wellness
57	Chapter 11:	Four Components of 360 Cultural Leadership

Part 2

61	Chapter 12:	Success Wellness
67	Chapter 13:	Social Wellness
73	Chapter 14:	Value Wellness
79	Chapter 15:	Cultural Wellness
85	Chapter 16:	Intellectual Wellness
91	Chapter 17:	Emotional Wellness
97	Chapter 18:	Physical Wellness
103	Chapter 19:	Environmental Wellness

Part 3

109	Chapter 20:	New Preschool Ideas
113	Chapter 21:	Social Change For POWER Teachers
119	Chapter 22:	Rationale For Developing Cultural Leaders
125	Chapter 23:	Preparing Students For Success
131	Chapter 24:	360 CL, Holism, Scholar Assessments, Process-based Learning, Performance-based Learning

Part 4

135	Chapter 25:	Connecting Excellence, Culture, Marginalization, Support, Preschoolers, and Experts
147	Chapter 26:	Teaching Leadership Versus Punitive Reactionary Actions
153	References:	

Introduction

Researchers, teachers, and parents all over the world have studied the concept of school failure and asked why school systems are failing such a great number of students. I am in the class of academic skeptics; in particular, I had to find answers to the dilemma of preschool expulsion. A former school administrator once asserted that children are not failing; instead, we are failing our children. Many factors can cause school systems to fail students school politics, "good old boy" networks, teacher burnout, marginalization of teachers, low salaries for teachers, too many standards and tests, outdated assessment practices, consistent achievement gaps, persistent and inequitable practices, and student disengagement. Few, if any, of these identified factors are caused by the students.

My concern for my students mounted year after year. Every day, I questioned how to help my students. I began to look for any type of solution that would help. While looking for answers, I began to ask teachers and students why they believed students were failing in such large numbers. Teachers thought students were apathetic and lazy; students said they were bored. Teachers often blamed teachers of students in the lower grades for not doing their due diligence to prepare students; students said that most teachers didn't care. Teachers blamed the lack of parental concern as a major problem that hindered student achievement. Clearly, there was plenty of blame to go around. At that point in my teaching career, I embarked on a research journey to identify the real problem. Finding solutions began much like following breadcrumbs: the answer led me to preschool. I found that preschool data eerily mirrored and reflected societal punitive practices. I concluded the foundation, the beginning of students' academic journey, is crumbling. Part of the problem lies in preschool.

At the beginning of my teaching career, I did not connect preschool to middle school. However, every journey begins with questions. I questioned why so many African American boys were failing horribly in mathematics. I questioned why so many African American boys were in special education classes. I questioned why so few minority students were in gifted classes.

Many experiences influenced me during my journey. One experience in particular involved an African American boy who came to class every single day but never participated. I tried to reach him using any strategy I could think of. Through relationship development and many conversations, I came to understand that his reading level was very low. I thought about the pain of his mathematic journey. These feelings of helplessness made me research a myriad of strategies; and led me to write my first book, *Ethnoacademics: 5 Secret Strategies for Teaching Black Boys Academic Success*. I used mathematic lessons in my book and wrote them in the form of a play. Mathematic scripts allow low-level readers to become part of the mathematic lesson. Teachers assign small reading roles to low-level readers, while more advanced readers read parts that require more fluency delivery. Mathematic scripts allow for many roles, multiple roles allow teachers to include all students in the process. Having roles for all levels of readers is one methodology to use when trying to engage all students in mathematics.

I remembered students' statements about being bored. After much research on theories and methodologies that might work for disengaged students, I began to look into the use of project-based learning and found that it can work well for a broad spectrum of students; however, it was not the academic game changer I thought it would be. Outside community life, difficult family life, poverty, and low literacy skills proved to be part of a formula that leads to mass failure, particularly in mathematics. As my students moved to high school, new problems began to emerge. I saw my students' names mentioned in news about breaking and entering, carjackings, drug dealing, murder, and a double homicide. Students were moving from the school system straight to the prison system. As if the above incidents were not heart breaking enough, I had another student killed in a bad drug deal and another who died of a heroin overdose.

Once again, I had to look for answers. I saw signs of students dealing with emotional and inequality issues. Why were students' literacy levels so low? This educational dike was full of holes and leaking like a sieve, but I had to find out when the leaks had begun. That's when I started to look at the preschooler. I had often thought that students' academic careers begin in Kindergarten, but I was wrong. I did not realize that preschool has become the new Kindergarten. I discovered that preschool issues are muddled with issues witnessed in society. African American boys are expelled from preschool in large numbers, researchers report that urban children do not have the vocabulary of their affluent counterparts, and children as young as 3 and 4 years of age are experiencing violence and participating in violent acts. A Google search will produce articles on these young children being involved in gun violence. Punitive practices in the preschool setting are taking a toll on preschoolers.

I tried to imagine how human beings who have been in this world for just 3 or 4 years could handle feelings of frustration, marginalization, and socioemotional challenges. Preschoolers in punitive learning environments begin to develop manipulative and dishonest practices. Preschoolers also begin to exhibit habits and behaviors that make them susceptible to negative actions that can be witnessed in middle and high school. Negative middle and high school actions that can be witnessed include a propensity for alcohol and drug abuse, engage in delinquency practices, have lower academic scores and less literacy success, and are prone to become bullies if they live in punitive and aggressive environments that hasten the feelings of helplessness. Many of these young children are doomed to lives of despair.

All educational systems should affirm the humanity of preschoolers. Teaching children who belong to other people is a job unlike any other. Teachers are charged with making sure children are advancing academically. However, the job of teaching also entails a complex mixture of parent, social worker, nurse, and psychologist. The latest absurd expectation is that teachers now must be gunslingers.

Teachers must become astute in many areas that are outside their content specialties. Teachers are expected to have the skills to assess their own learning requirements so that they can understand the learning styles of their students. Teachers must learn patterns associated with all students in order to fulfill educational obligations. But wait, there's more: Teachers also must understand a myriad of cultures (school, students, and society).

When teachers start their careers, they don't normally give culture a great deal of thought. However, the lack of understanding culture has resulted in certain groups of students to struggle, and for many students, this struggle begins in preschool. Over the past 10 years, researchers have tried to stress the inequitable processes that exist for African American students that begin in preschool. African American preschoolers are expelled and suspended more often than their peers. In fact, preschoolers are expelled and suspended more than k-12th grade students. Walter S. Gilliam, a Yale professor, is among the researchers who have tried to explain the classroom practices that are hindering the academic and socioemotional progress of African American preschool boys.

Teachers' perceptions of preschoolers ages 3 and 4 years have a profound effect on how these youngsters develop academically, socially, and emotionally. One of the most important pieces of data garnered from the Yale studies stated that when teachers and their students are from the same racial background, there are fewer suspensions and expulsions. Previous research also has made it clear that when teachers and preschoolers are from different racial backgrounds, academic complications often persist. One of the major and most damaging complications is the rate of expulsion for African American children. African American boys once held the top place in expulsions and suspensions, but African American girls are fast approaching the out-of-class time of their male counterparts.

There are grave consequences to preschool expulsion. One of the most egregious consequences is the slow decline in the academic promise of 3- and 4-year-old preschoolers. The slow erosion of confidence in the classroom, feelings of unworthiness, and all of the negative self-describing terms that preschoolers will develop about who they are will persist. The term *push-out phenomenon* has come to describe inequitable preschool practices. Monique W. Morris explicitly described the push-out process as it related to African American girls in her book, *Pushout: The Criminalization of Black Girls in Schools*. The data in the book brought this crisis into stark reality. Yale researchers quantified the reality that African American children make up 19% of preschool enrollment yet make up 47% of suspended preschoolers. There can be no argument that these findings are shocking, unpleasant, and disheartening. Action must be taken to help all students to achieve academic success.

Researchers have identified preschool as the new educational focus. Although preschool was once considered a choice for many parents, it has become an essential ungrade for parents to consider. Politicians, academics, and teachers no longer consider preschool an option. Parents often find the cost of preschool as prohibitive, leaving their children unable to participate in the process. A significant number of single parents, married couples, and grandparents find the cost unrealistic. Affordable preschool might not provide the academic rigor and high quality needed to ensure that children are prepared for Kindergarten. The notion of high-quality preschool is not a new concept;

wealthy couples have placed their children in high-quality preschools for decades. Preschools with rigor have as their mission the preparation of student greatness, but poorer families often rely on grandparents to watch their children. The importance of grandparents' love and support are not at issue in this book. What is at issue is the role of inequality in preschool education.

Wealthy families pay tuitions that range from $30,000 to $50,000 a year for preschool. It should not go unnoticed that such an education will provide academic and collaborative relationships that will benefit their children for years to come. Families that do not have the luxury of enriched preschool or influential connections might not realize that their children need skills beyond reading, writing, and mathematics. Success in the 21st century will require providing all students with a broad set of skills and opportunities to apply these skills. If education is considered the social equalizer, then policy changes related to curriculum and teachers' salaries should be more proactive. It is clear that money plays a large part in the type of education children receive. Providing a leadership teaching approach in preschool will help preschoolers develop skills needed to handle robust education requirements. How will educational systems provide this type of education? What will it look like? Will all preschoolers have access to this type of education?

All children have the right to an excellent education. In order for this to happen, revisioning must take place. Uncomfortable issues like diversity, beliefs about poverty, beliefs about wealth, teachers' reflections, content delivery, and underfunding all play a huge role in the education of preschoolers who come from poorer families. The United States pays lip service to the education of preschoolers by not providing the funding needed to level the academic playing field as it relates to child care costs and the low salaries of preschool teachers.

If we recognize and acknowledge that 3-year-old children are operating at a peak stage of brain development, then it seems prudent and proactive to establish and implement a course of study to support all students. All families of children ages 3 and 4 years should be able to take advantage of this period of children's cognitive growth. The gap between rich and poor is widening, and not much has been invested in preschool education. The United States lags far behind other developed countries in preschool preparedness.

What is being offered in affluent preschool that is not being offered in other preschools? How can poorer preschools begin to compete with affluent preschools? If our students are the product of our teaching, then what and how should we teach them so they can have successful lives? What should our students be able to change in their environments? Society's current views and practices are being reflected in our preschools. These social norms are having a detrimental effect on all children, regardless of ethnicity or cultural or economic background. For example, the punitive practices seen in the adult justice system are being seen and enforced in our preschools. Bias in preschools must be addressed. Biased practices in preschool have long-term negative effects on preschoolers, and we have no way of knowing how deeply such biased practices will change the relationships that preschoolers will have with future academic success. Culture, bias, poverty, inequality, and a lack of resources are components of the negative trajectory facing marginalized preschoolers. I propose we develop a system that will help too dramatically improve the lives of preschoolers. Teaching teachers to teach cultural leadership skills to preschoolers might be the solution to the long-term challenge of negative preschool outcomes.

One way to deal with inequality is through learning about and teaching cultural leadership skills. In order for this to happen, our students need to be taught leadership skills right from their preschool days. Leadership skills have not been explicitly taught in any grade. The struggles and successes of prominent leaders and what these leaders have done throughout our history have been studied, but connecting our students to their own leadership potential has not. Many students never consider leadership as it relates to who they are; rarely is there an academic connection for students to see who they are or can be as leaders and scholars. Children see their teachers, parents, police, principals, and other family members as leaders. As students progress through the educational system to high school, they will either participate in or witness voting for a class president, but many students do not even know why being class president is important. Students don't often think about their own leadership attributes, so teaching leadership skills should be an important goal. Students are not taught how to be leaders in their own lives.

Preschoolers are overwhelmed with media that promote competition, not cooperation, cohesiveness, and empathy. The intent of this book is to convince teachers, school administrators, and politicians that all students, rich or poor, can be educated with excellence. Providing a system of excellence in cultural leadership that is easy to duplicate and works within the confines of the mandated curriculum is essential.

If preschools reflect what is happening in society relevant to stereotyping and taking punitive actions against marginalized groups, then high expulsion rates and suspensions for preschoolers will continue. Without interventions, the rates of expulsion and suspension for African American boys will continue to rise higher than for other preschool children. Without interventions, African American girls and Hispanic American boys will share out-of-school suspensions that are similar to those being experienced by their African American male peers.

Preschool discipline mirrors the elementary and high school discipline structures that have been accused of supporting the preschool-to-prison pipeline system. These punitive structures were designed to feed the prison population. The marginalization of some preschoolers can begin in preschool, with some students lagging behind their counterparts. If school systems continue to reflect negative social practices, targeted students will follow negative social paths. We have two choices: We either begin to arrest preschoolers or we teach them leadership skills.

My last research endeavor focused on culture, leadership, and systems. I realized that to ensure that students have a chance to thrive in their school systems, a system that addresses culture, socioemotional concerns, wellness, academics, inequality, and leadership needs to be created. I developed a system that I call 360 Cultural Leadership (360CL). While studying school systems, it occurred to me that we are operating with Newtonian ideas, ideas that operate in bits and pieces and not in a cohesive, purposeful system that promotes success for all students. 360CL system has as its design the study of what makes students successful. It is my opinion that what is needed to promote success, excellence, and leadership is a system that can operate within the realm of holism. Educational holism will provide students with academic practices that promote the uniqueness of all students. Newtonian practices require the study of many bits and pieces of the academic system; however, studying parts and pieces will not provide what is needed to make the whole system work effectively. Many needed academic, cultural, and social-emotional parts and pieces do not get infused in the system; when this happens marginalized students are further disadvantaged. Educational systems must meet the needs of the whole child and all students.

My hope is that after you read this book, you will consider the importance of teaching students 360CL skills, wellness foundations, and skills that extend beyond the three content areas of reading, writing, and arithmetic. Cultural leadership needs a system in which to operate, a foundation in which to survive, and the willingness of teachers to implement the program. Teaching 360CL skills to our children will give them, their families, their schools, and their communities lifelong benefits. The purpose of this book is to help our marginalized preschoolers.

Above all, remember that LOVE is all we need. Make sure your work is fun.

Chapter 1

Why Do We Need A Cultural Leadership Workbook?

> A leader is one who knows the way, goes the way and shows the way.
> John Maxwell

OBJECTIVES

- ✓ Understand why cultural differences are complex.
- ✓ Guide teachers to explore their beliefs.
- ✓ Help teachers understand the connection between academic success and wellness.
- ✓ Clarify the importance of competencies and wellness domains.

Many teachers who work in diverse classrooms are often engaged in cultural mismatches and often face academic and social challenges. Unfortunately, teachers who wittingly or unwittingly make stereotypical assumptions about their students find it difficult to get the academic outcomes they expect and desire. Cultural teacher leaders are needed more than ever; however, studying culture cannot be the end goal. The end goal is to make sure we are teaching students in an environment of excellence. Classroom cultural myopia has continued to shred the integrity of the academic lives of many students. Cultural differences can lead to complexities in communication and expectations; according to Louis et al. (2010), educators and policymakers should create leadership programs that support instruction. This workbook was designed to help preschool teachers to incorporate leadership competencies and domains into daily instruction.

This workbook was created to help preschool teachers understand and implement a system of cultural leadership. It can be a guide for novice and experienced teachers to help them develop a language of cultural effectiveness, leadership, academics, and social skills development. Teachers differ in the way they teach so the domains and competencies are defined; however, the teacher and teacher teams will be responsible for how they wish to incorporate the system. With planning and spending time with the workbook and applying the simple system, teachers might find the system makes a difference in the future of their students. There are three concepts that will be address in the workbook.

First, you will explore information about who you are. You need to know what kind of teacher leader you would like to be. You need to know whether you are able to accomplish what you wish in your classroom with what you already practice and know. Of course if you are unfamiliar with the system you will have time to learn the concepts in your own time or with your team of teachers. Second, you need information about the connections between culture and education. You will learn how to incorporate leadership concepts into your daily work. You will develop knowledge and skills that will be easy to incorporate. Third, you need to know if your teacher training has prepared you to teach in diverse classrooms.

This workbook will help you learn about the spectrum of wellness domains that are used to help facilitate and create a learning environment of academic excellence. 360CL will also help teachers develop a plan of action to improve teacher cultural effectiveness. There are eight competencies and eight domains that are used as the framework foundation. In order to learn more about the relationship between competencies, domains and student wellness we will begin by examining our own ideas of teacher leadership, then we will move deeper into the system. Cultural leadership implementation into the classroom will help prepare all students to be leaders in their own life and in the lives of others. Preschoolers are remarkable amazing little people, POWER Preschool teacher are the answer to help change the way we help children learn how to think deeply. The first step will be in developing a common language for SCHOLAR.

Chapter 2

What's In The Name SCHOLAR? Our Greatest Product

I am a great scholar; my mind is full of wonders.

Lailah Gifty Akita

OBJECTIVE

✓ Understand how to define SCHOLAR.

A scholar has been defined as one who has done advanced studies in a special field, or a person who studies under a teacher (Merriam-*Webster Dictionary Online Dictionary*, 2018). We are accustomed to seeing the word scholar, and most of us have an idea about what we believe the word scholar means. However, for the purpose of cultural leadership development, SCHOLAR is defined as a preschoolers who can:

Successfully

Choose

Habits of

Ownership that

Lead to

Advanced

Readiness.

Defining SCHOLAR is important because it helps teachers and students understand the actions that are attached to the word. We say that we want students to be successful, but what is success?

Success

Success language means infusing the language of success into everyday teaching strategies. Success language plants seeds of success during daily activities of preschoolers. Teachers should be responsible for helping students understand what success is, provide opportunities for students to feel successful, and model and provide examples of what success means to others.

How would we define a successful year for preschoolers? What skills would we implement to ensure that our preschools have a successful year? Before reading my list, perhaps you might want to make your own list of what you believe successful preschoolers have achieved after their first year of preschool. I have included a few of my ideas below:

- ✓ I consider preschoolers successful if immersion and participation in a learning environment that is robust and filled with performance centers.

- ✓ I consider preschoolers successful if they can master writing their full name.

- ✓ I consider preschoolers successful if they are learning how to become fluent readers.

- ✓ I consider preschoolers successful if they have learned 73 sight words.

- ✓ I consider preschoolers successful if they own at least 10 books.

- ✓ I consider preschoolers successful if they learn that differences are natural and fantastic.

Of course, teachers will provide their own list of what success should be. I would suggest preschool centers help define what they wish for their students to achieve during a day; however, they can also be used to track progress after a month, or a year. Create a <u>Success Tracker</u> form. After a year, you will be able to track and copy the <u>Success Tracker</u> form for parents. In the space below, design a **<u>Success Tracker</u>**. You will need pencils and markers.

Choice

Choosing or teaching students how to choose happens when teachers give students options for action scenarios. For example, if students decide to listen to bad advice from other students, they might find themselves in trouble because of that decision. Such a scenario is the perfect opportunity to discuss choices and consequences. Schwartz (2009) posited that a good way for students to begin to understand choice is for them to develop a clear understanding of their goals. Preschoolers should have the opportunity in the course of their day to make informed choices. Preschoolers might not know how to set goals. Teachers will have to model the concept of attaining goals and making choices. A weekly goal can be established and tracked. It is important to use the term *goal* when preparing students to become scholars.

Establish a Goal and Offer Choices

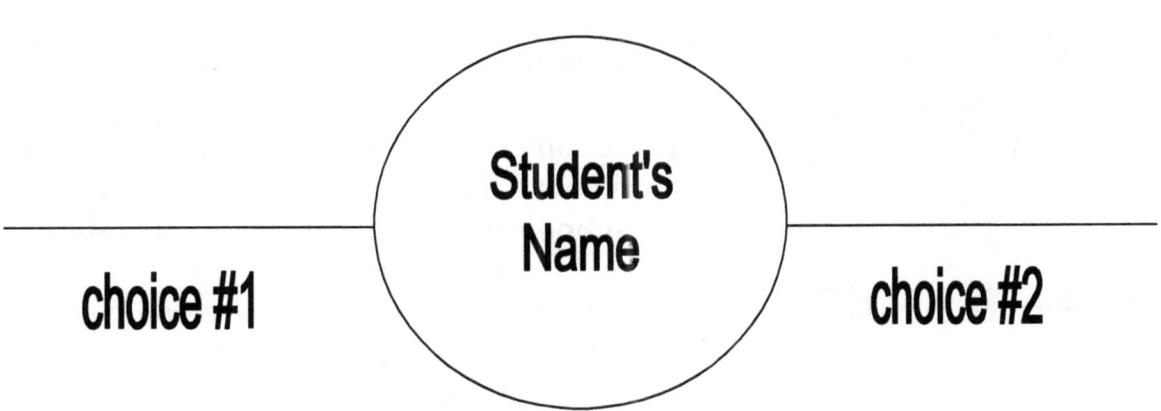

Habits

Habits related to being scholarly are behavioral sequences aimed to promote intentional choices. Habits can be negative or positive; however, we are emphasizing positive habits that will lead to goal attainment when they are practiced. According to Wood and Neal (2007), habits are formed when intentional and established patterns become a process that benefits a particular goal. In order to facilitate habits, actions that are performed on a regular basis become so familiar, the habit can be formed without conscious effort (Jog, Kubota, Connolly, Hillegaart, & Graybiel, 1999). Covey (2013) introduced us to *7 Habits of Highly Effective People*. Although I don't expect teachers to become followers of any particular person, the seven habits are established behaviors that will benefit preschoolers. Covey connected habits to character, stating that habits are a composite of character. Seven habits are detailed in his book; however, for our purpose, we wish to introduce preschoolers to the concept of habitual language. A synopsis of the seven habits follows:

Habit # 1	Be Proactive	**Preschoolers** learn it is fine to make mistakes. They will begin to understand responsibility
Habit #2	Begin with the End in Mind	**Preschoolers** will learn how to plan.
Habit # 3	Put First Things First	**Preschoolers** will learn to develop self-control.
Habit # 4	Seek to Understand then to be understood	**Preschoolers** will learn the art of listening.
Habit # 5	Think Win/Win	**Preschoolers** will have the opportunity to learn how it feels to communicate positively.
Habit # 6	Synergize	**Preschoolers** begin providing solutions to classroom social challenges.
Habit # 7	Sharpen the Saw	**Preschoolers** participate in opportunities to explore mental, physical, social-emotional, and wholeness activities.

Ownership

Ownership in scholarly pursuits means students make no excuses for their successes and failures. Guiding students to practice solving these challenges happens over time. Ownership and not making excuses could be one of the hardest skills preschoolers face. Preschoolers often believe mistakes mean something bad, or bullying others to get your needs met is the way to go, and sharing is not that great of an activity. Of course, they are learning how to behave socially. We want our preschoolers to begin being aware of the importance of their academics. Helping students become aware of the reasons academics are important to them is the first skill needed for preschool ownership. In this case, the use of process-based skills development could be helpful. For example, as children begin to write their names and form letters, we want them to be cognizant of neatness. Helping preschoolers develop mastery skills is part of the ownership we want them to obtain.

Preschool teachers help preschoolers learn how to work through difficult social, cultural, and academic situations. Preschool ownership refers to helping students do their best every day and feel pride in at least one event for the day. Preschool ownership of learning lies in the form of engagement. Conley and French (2014) offered three components of engagement teachers should be cognizant of:

Behavioral Engagement	Preschoolers will be monitored to determine how they are engaging in the norms and expectations of the classroom and school benefit behavior.
Cognitive Engagement	Preschoolers will be monitored to determine if they are being challenged in their classrooms.
Emotional Engagement	Preschoolers should be monitored to help to determine if they are interested in their activities and enjoy the work they perform.

Helping preschoolers to develop ownership of their learning will require close monitoring.

Leads to

Advanced	in the 21st century, means that students are provided opportunities to use content-area skills in real-world situations. Process-based learning is one way to build skills needed to think critically, develop solutions, and execute student work beyond worksheets.

Readiness	is what teachers should see as preschoolers leave their class and move on to kindergarten. There should be more than test scores to ensure parents and the community that students are ready for future academic and personal engagements.

Twelve years a SCHOLAR. We will have our fantastic students for approximately 12 years. Preparing students to become global leaders should be the goal. We know that we must educate the whole child. In Chapter 4, we develop a common language to define "whole child.

Chapter 3

Why Teach Preschoolers Leadership?

*If your actions inspire others to dream more, learn more,
do more and become more, you are a leader.*

John Quincy Adams

OBJECTIVES

- ✓ Identify the importance of self-awareness.
- ✓ Identify teacher leadership.
- ✓ Identify teacher POWER.

Now that we have defined what preschool SCHOLARs should be, we will begin to explore how to get them to a point of success. The first step will be to help preschool teachers become POWER preschool teachers. Proof of Work Engagement and Retention (POWER) teachers learn how to become culturally effective by being able to prove how their work is engaging and how students retain and use content. To move teachers to the POWER point, we need to address teachers' awareness. Perceptions of preschool teachers have been changing slowly; in the past, preschool teachers were underpaid and not always thought of as "true" teachers. Parts of society think of preschool teachers as no more than glorified babysitters and not educated professionals. Preschool educators in the global education community are paid a respectable monetary value for their work; preschool teachers in the United States are grossly underpaid.

Besides the low rate of pay for preschool teachers, two other identified areas are hindering teachers from becoming POWER teachers. Many teachers have to work other jobs, and some find the stress of working more than one job distressing. The other obstacle that might hinder preschool teachers from becoming POWER teachers could be the absence of a teaching framework. POWER teachers become powerful because they gain appropriate background knowledge to understand the importance of their teacher leadership. When teachers are aware of the power of their leadership and understand what that concept really means, they are able to ensure that all students are learning in an academically rich environment. We will explore what teacher leaders are and what type of system needs to be in place not only to improve their teaching framework but also to improve or change how teachers think about their leadership. Organizing preschoolers around an identity of teacher leadership provide a strong academic identity in which to work.

In her book, *Leadership and the New Science* Margaret J. Wheatley eloquently described how leadership skills could improve the power of teachers. She stated there is no need for an individual to be part of a large number of people to make changes in a system. Teachers can be influential teacher leaders. Teachers can use their influence to become that small disturbance that can amplify through networks effectively. Wheatley also stated that once the disturbance is operating within the system, the network amplifies, and change is witnessed.

The rest of the book describes the framework and the application of a cultural leadership system. As stated earlier, awareness is the first step in the amplification of teaching cultural leadership. The first concept of awareness is the examination of our own leadership thoughts. There are no right or wrong answers; your honest answers will help to gauge your actions and impact in the classroom. Are you a teacher who's a leader or a leader who's a teacher? What type of leader are you? Have you thought about leading for intellectual and social change? If yes, explain; if no, explain.

It is essential to explore awareness primarily because our thoughts define our behaviors and actions. Awareness also involves exploring how students affect our thoughts, behaviors, and actions; teachers must be honest about their communicative practices and expectations related to all students. Teachers must examine their thoughts to determine if they have negative thoughts about a student or groups of students, if negative thoughts exist, the teacher must examine why they harbor such thoughts. Once teachers define their thoughts, beliefs, and views, then defining their expectations for all students will be part of the move to excellence. After exploring our self-awareness, then we will be able to define what we believe a whole child is and understand how we can connect to the idea of SCHOLAR.

1. *Quick Synopsis Work:* Are you a teacher who's a leader or a leader who's a teacher?

   _____

   _____

   _____

   _____

2. *Quick Synopsis Work:* Describe your type of leadership.

   _____

   _____

   _____

   _____

3. *Quick Synopsis Work:* Have you thought about leading for intellectual and social change?

   _____

   _____

   _____

   _____

4. Quick Synopsis Work: If your answer to #3 is yes, explain below. If your answer to #3 is no, explain below.

_____

_____

_____

_____

_____

_____

_____

_____

_____

_____

Chapter 4

360 Whole Child*ism*

We believe success of each learner can only be achieved through a whole-child approach to learning and teaching.

Dr. Gene Carter

OBJECTIVES

- ✓ Define whole child *ism*.
- ✓ Define holism.
- ✓ Define the importance of a system.

Holism concepts and theories are used to shape the archetype of the whole child in order to have a common language about what defines the whole child. Child*ism* uses child as the system, practice, and philosophy. Holism was defined by Smuts (1926) as the tendency in nature to form wholes that are greater than the sum of the parts through creative evolution. My hope is that by using a holistic systematic approach, more students will achieve academic and personal success. Educational holism is defined and framed by an ecological approach, and consists of competencies and domains. Educational holism is concerned with the total development of the student. Social, academic, personal, leadership, and socioemotional components will be brought together systematically in order to ensure that students are prepared to meet the societal and academic needs of the 21st century. Systematic approaches help to implement the process of student development in a way that does not impose undue challenges on teachers.

Addressing the whole child requires analyzing a spectrum of individual complexity. Part of educational experiences should address who students are or are trying to be while cultivating inner relationships and outer environmental relationships. Students' experiences should also provide a way to give all students the strength and ability to build confidence. Theoretical holism language is a powerful combination of concepts that work interchangeably to support academic goals. If synergy between academic and personal concepts is not achieved, many students will continue to have negative school experiences.

Practitioners of holistic education hope to challenge the fragmentation of the Cartesian-Newtonian view and practices of education. This particular model of education pays homage to bits and pieces of structures and ideas, but identifying or defining the nature of a fragmented system is difficult because there is usually not a systemic purpose other than the wishes of stakeholders. Holistic education seeks to transform the ways education systems are implemented so that all students will develop their own self-leadership.

Educational holism uses system components to determine how the whole system can be used to benefit all students. The whole system determines how the parts will behave and benefit students. Educational holism focuses on the interconnectedness of the competencies and domains, students' experiences, and real-world situations. Developing the pedagogy of the system is essential to ensuring that teachers can implement 360CL without being frustrated. Instructional techniques cannot be isolated and unrelated; rather, if implementation is cemented in the larger vision of students as SCHOLARs, students will have a better chance for success.

Quick Synopsis Work: Detail and define what your organization's beliefs are about what it means to educate the whole child. Identify what you have in place to defend your answers.

_____

_____

_____

_____

_____

_____

_____

_____

_____

_____

Chapter 5

Culture, Teaching And The Academic Relationship

Education can change culture but only in so far as educators are transformed.

Parent School Board

OBJECTIVES

- ✓ Understand the importance of cultures in education.
- ✓ Explore the possibilities of implementing a cultural system.
- ✓ Help teachers understand cultural mismatches.

Culture determines how we behave, think, speak, and feel. Culture is responsible for shaping our identity and influencing how we interact with our families, classmates, and community. Perspectives on global and social issues are part of the landscape of how people engage in dialogue and communicate. Culture is complicated and multilayered, so defining all the nuances of culture is difficult. Culture and cultural pride are innate to everyone. Knowledge from family culture helps humans to adapt and maneuver through their lives. However, when teachers, support staff, and administrators who are in charge of educating culturally diverse groups of children don't share the same culture as the students, cultural mismatches often occur and produce barriers to delivering academic content and maintaining discipline.

Defining Culture in Education

Culture is not difficult to understand; instead, the difficulty comes from the broad interpretation and use of the term, such as school culture, teacher culture, community culture, family culture, or the culture of girls and boys in middle school. Culture, the ways that groups think, dress, act, eat, and worship, is part of the human experience. Education systems must:

1. Understand what type of culture they are trying to develop.
2. Be honest about the culture they have developed.
3. Be willing to create practical action steps that improve the culture in the learning environment for students and teachers.

Developing and implementing a cultural leadership system that runs parallel to curriculum, standards and norms have the purpose of changing the behavioral patterns of students and teachers. Culture in education often is defined by common ideas, desired behaviors, academic goals, wellness goals, differentiation of student skills, social identity, and school leadership goals.

The purpose of creating and implementing an educational culture is to ensure that all students have a sense of belonging in their learning environment. Researchers have determined that students who feel a sense of belonging and inclusion perform better in their academic endeavors. Discussing culture is difficult for adults. However, conversations about culture must happen to move and transform classroom norms. Professional development must be meaningful, and teachers must be able to work in an environment that listens to all teachers' perspectives. To prepare students for 21st-century success, education systems should support the development of meta-cognitive competencies as early as preschool.

Quick Synopsis Work: Define your ideas of culture.

Chapter 6

Exploring The Culture Of The Whole Child

Education's purpose is to replace an empty mind with an open one.

Malcolm S. Forbes

OBJECTIVES

- ✓ Understand the meaning of the whole child.
- ✓ Connect across interdisciplinary content.
- ✓ Help teachers begin to think culturally.

Educators are taught about the importance of educating the whole child; however, many curriculum models and strategies have failed to implement diversity in the content. Although more students from diverse cultural and socioeconomic backgrounds are populating our classrooms; their cultures are noticeably absent from many of the pedagogical approaches that address the whole of who these diverse students are. Culture that represents the whole child has barely expanded from the idea of diversity that mostly addresses boys and girls, and Black and White students. Super and Harkness (1986) identified three components that are necessary to understand cultural efficiency;

1.	the importance of having physical and social awareness of students' cultures;
2.	being aware of children's cultural customs related to child development; and
3.	the mental thought of the teacher.

Children's individual development will depend on teachers implementing culture across interdisciplinary content; effective cultural models have social change elements that are infused in the lessons. Teachers' challenge to identify a broader array of cultures as well as know how to ensure an inclusive curriculum that represents all students in all content areas is the goal. Classroom teachers must be aware of and accommodate not only ethnic differences but also gender diversity. Whatever the identified teachers challenge, culture in the classroom must represent all students if the goal is to prepare all students to be successful in the 21st century. Cultural forces influence the psychology of the child (Kessen, (1979). Students feel compelled to become more involved in their own futures when acknowledging their cultures is seen as being important and when their cultures are connected to their academic outcomes. Garrett (2006) warned that teachers have a responsibility to ensure students are taught social skills; however, many researchers have supported the inclusion of social skills, but have not considered childrens' cultures as necessary.

Quick Synopsis Work: Write three reasons for exploring culture in the classroom.

Chapter 7

The System: Domains And Competencies Of Cultural Leadership

Leaders must be close enough to relate to others, but far enough ahead to motivate them.

John C. Maxwell

OBJECTIVES

- ✓ Understand cultural competencies.
- ✓ Understand a cultural system.

Cultural teacher leaders (CTL) prepare students to become self-motivated learners who take the initiative to explore and promote their academic and personal destinies. Competencies are what students should be able to do or have the ability to accomplish. Cultural leadership competencies are arranged around the concept of personal leadership. Teachers' expectations or intentions are to have students become self-regulated. Cultural leadership's program design operates with the teaching design methodology focusing on the identified domains and competencies. One way that teachers can help students to become their own leaders is by following a system. The cultural leadership framework includes eight domains and eight competencies.

For students to become productive and fully functional adults who are in control of making decisions that promote personal wellness, they need to develop more than just academic mastery. Researchers have reported that businesses are in short supply of competent workers; colleges have determined that a great number of students are taking remedial classes because they are not ready to be successful in college. If 21st-century skills do not include skills development in self-management, collaboration, and leadership, then many students will not be prepared to function as workers, college students, or entrepreneurs.

Many teachers understand the importance of students receiving affective skills development; however, many teachers also feel overwhelmed and are not anxious to assume more responsibilities. Researchers have continued to stress the importance of providing students with preparation tools that can be useful in school and adulthood. CTLs use a conceptual model with four domains: interpersonal; intrapersonal; leadership; and academic, workforce, and entrepreneurial (AWE) skills. Domains are broad identifiable concepts linked to specific goals. The goal of CTLs is to provide all of the tools necessary for students to be successful. The 21st-century knowledge base is shifting from skills to competencies, so teachers need a framework that helps them to incorporate domains and competencies into the curriculum. Eight competencies correspond to four leadership types; the competencies are identifies as; (a) listening; (b) empathy; (c) self-belief; (d) confidence; (e) attitude; (f) discipline; (g) failure; and (h) awareness. The following framework of domains corresponds to the competencies.

Four Cultural Leadership Types and Eight Competencies

Intrapersonal	Interpersonal	Leadership	AWE
Success/Culture	Environmental/Social	Intellectual/Physical and Mental	Value/Emotional
Related competencies	**Related competencies**	**Related competencies**	**Related competencies**
Listening	Empathy	Attitude	Self-Belief
Confidence	Awareness	Failure	Discipline

Chapter 8

Cultural Leadership Competencies

Becoming a leader is synonymous with becoming yourself.
It is precisely that simple and it is also that difficult.
Warren Bennis

OBJECTIVES

- ✓ Understand the importance of cultural leadership.
- ✓ Guide teachers in to become cultural leadership ambassadors.
- ✓ Help teachers understand the process of leadership.

It is never too early to teach leadership. In fact, modeling leadership and providing opportunities for children to learn what it takes to be a leader is more important today than any other time in modern history. If society begins to accept egregious acts from leaders as being acceptable, then teaching the importance of leadership might become difficult. Many leadership representatives of today show little regard for the lives of people that live in poverty, suffer with mental and physical challenges, or work two and three jobs just too barely survive. Providing leadership training for preschoolers is essential. When children learn how to work within the leadership program, and begin to develop strong positive characteristics, over time they will develop skills that will help them navigate through difficult situations. Part of the leadership training includes helping children to develop thoughts that can improve their lives. Getting the most out of leadership training requires immersing children in the process of academics and leadership. Learning how to apply thoughts to overcome life challenges is the goal. Educators have the opportunity to change or shape new groups of leader. Characteristics like empathy, listening, and compassion can be introduced and provided a space to be bracketed in a education and leadership system.

Competency #1: Listening

Grassroots organizations form because they have a mission they feel passionate about; Tarana Burke began the Me Too Movement to make people aware of the seriousness of sexual harassment and assaults. For any movement to gain traction, one needs to collect a group of **active listeners**.

Cultural Leadership Teaches That: Students must know that **listening** skills are one of the most important skills needed to be successful in the 21st century.

Competency #2: Empathy

We do not want our children to accept ridicule of individuals with handicaps as a normal human reaction to those that are different. Instead, we want our children to build **empathy** into their mental academic program.

Cultural Leadership Teaches That: Students must know that the ability to understand and share the feelings of others is **empathy**.

Competency #3: Self-Beliefs

Alaska's ice is melting at an alarming rate; videos and reports from archeologists detail the negative effect of global warming on our global community. Despite the increasing evidence of the melting ice, some people still believe there is no such thing as global warming. Students must be taught how to examine their **self-beliefs** in order to know how to make informed decisions.

Cultural Leadership Teaches That: Students must know **self-beliefs** are built on thoughts, strengths, and weaknesses; they must know how to improve on underdeveloped skills.

Competency #4: Confidence

Shaquem Griffin has worked diligently and consistently to make his dreams come true. He has been drafted too play for the Seattle Seahawks, the same team as his twin brother Shaquill Griffin. What makes his remarkable story so inspiring is the fact that he will play professional football with one hand. He could not have achieved his goals, dreams, and aspirations without **confidence**; fortunately, he never received the mental memo that informed all potential football players that they must have two hands to realize their dream of playing in a professional league.

Cultural Leadership Teaches That: Students must be taught the power of **confidence** and know ways to construct their own **confidence** tools.

Competency #5: Attitude

Rolihlahla Mandela was known throughout the world as Nelson Mandela. Nelson Mandela spent 27 years in jail because he dared to fight for the implementation of human rights in South Africa. When released, he possessed a positive **attitude**, becoming the first Black man to serve as the president of South Africa from 1994-1999.

Cultural Leadership Teaches That: Students must be cognizant of the importance of their **attitude** and the impact attitude has on their academic and personal success.

Competency #6: Discipline

In 2014 LeBron James embarked on a 67-day quest to explore and participate in a Paleo diet. There was speculation that he was following the diet to improve his basketball game. The truth of the matter, as described by LeBron, was that he wanted to win another war of **discipline**. The 67 days of Paleo proved successful for LeBron; he proved that he owned his discipline and that his outside environment did not own him.

Cultural Leadership Teaches That: Students must know that **discipline** gives them control of their futures; either they learn how to be disciplined and control their own lives or they let others influence and control their destiny.

Competency #7: Failure

Motown, an American music company, chose its hits by way of having a group either approve or disapprove a song. The songs that **failed** provided important information about what not to do in other songs; the failures provided more insight into what customers wanted.

Cultural Leadership Teaches That: Students need to know that **failure** can give them vital information about what they need to change in order to succeed.

Competency #8: Awareness

Stoneman Douglas High School became **aware** that many choices made by adult politicians benefited lobbyist groups and did not protect the lives of Americans. On February 14, 2018, the mass shooting at Stoneman Douglas High School sparked a wave of activism among high school students. Adolescents became **aware** of their power to foment change in the global society.

Cultural Leadership Teaches That: Students need to know that **awareness** means being cognizant of activities or things in their environment that might benefit or harm them.

A Real Life Example of Teaching Leadership

One of the best examples of witnessing the results of teaching leadership can be seen by watching Steve Kerr, who coaches his team so well that he hands over his clipboard during an NBA game. His players impressively take over coaching the team. . This is a must see for anyone that needs to see what it looks like when you train or coach leadership. Search the actions of Steve Kerr on YouTube please watch:

1. Golden State Warriors Players Coach Themselves Full Coverage 2018.02.12 vs. Suns Free
2. Stephen A. Smith on Warriors' coaching experiment: Who cares Suns were offended?

Steve Kerr showed what happens when a teacher or coach in this case, prepared and taught his players in a way that showed the power of teaching leadership. He turned over the clipboard, said a few words to the players, and then sent the players off to coach each other. That is what teaching leadership looks like. Students have the skills they need to lead their own lives and the lives of others.

Quick Synopsis Work: Recall and write an example of positive leadership you have witnessed.

_____

_____

_____

_____

_____

_____

_____

Chapter 9

Wellness, Leadership And Education

Health is a state of body. Wellness is a state of being.

J. Stanford

OBJECTIVES

- ✓ Understand wellness.
- ✓ Guide teachers in understanding academics and wellness.
- ✓ Help teachers understand the connection between academics and wellness.
- ✓ Clarify the importance of competencies and domains.

Competencies and domains define 360CL. Competencies are the behaviors teachers want students to master. Wellness domains are cognitive, affective, and psychomotor. Competencies and wellness domains in education systems cannot be introduced and practiced sporadically or in fragments and still be expected to have an academic impact. Instead, the competencies and wellness domains will cycle for 8 weeks and then recycle twice more throughout the school year. Each time students are introduced to domains and competencies they will have the opportunity to produce more skills and applicable connections to their curriculum and state standards. A robust leadership program will help stave off the debilitating consequences of inequality in education systems.

Inequality is complex. Wellness domains help to provide a social-emotional and academic foundation to help all students experience excellence in their education. It is vital to incorporate wellness domains into preschool education because the focus must be on systematically educating the whole child. Wellness domains in 360CL are governed by a transvaluative process of helping children in becoming who they are. Transvaluation is the process of implementing a change in academic values and practices; changing the way we value preschool education for all children should begin with a change in processes and values in the system. For many preschool education programs, the idea of using wellness domains along with specific competencies will be a change or transformation in preschool processes and academic system. Dalsgaard and Otto (2016) define the concept of transvaluation as the combination of individualism and the creation of values. 360 CL's offers a spectrum of specific wellness concepts needed to help produce individualism along with the exploration of values. For all students to be successful, wellness domains must be infused into daily classroom routines.

The importance of implementing wellness domains in the classroom cannot be understated. Presently, marginalized preschoolers are operating in spaces that seem to be the opposite of wellness. In fact, many preschoolers of color begin to understand their differences through the negative experiences they have in school. Preschoolers have not had the opportunity to fully develop their social skills; therefore, their actions in the classroom setting need to be understood and managed in ways that will produce positive outcomes. Teachers must begin to understand and apply constructive actions, not excessive punishment.

Teachers must begin to explore the nature of their perceptions related to differences. How do these perceptions influence the experience of the marginalized students? We have to look no further than nature to understand that differences are by design. Nature supports the beauty in being different. Nature models in splendid form the beauty in diversity. For example, there are over 300,000 species of flowers; although flowers have different shapes, colors, heights, widths, needs, and purposes, no particular flower is better or more important than any other flower. Nature provides a cornucopia of examples of diversity. We see diversity in clouds, dogs, cats, birds, spiders, oceans, mountains, and of course people. We need to take our understanding and diversity cues from nature; color, size, gender or any other thing that makes a person different should be recognized and celebrated for being different rather than using differences to demonize or marginalize groups of people that are different.

Undervaluing the lives of those in diverse groups has resulted in war, hunger, poverty, polluted waters, homelessness, greed, and avarice. When we do not seek to understand those that are different; we will mismanage diversity. Preschoolers, young 3 and 4 years old people who act out in class could display negative behavior because they are hungry, live in poverty, drink from polluted waters, are homeless, mentally neglected, fearful, or feel marginalized. If students come to school and face punitive practices that mirror the ideology and practices of those witnessed in society and in the justice system students will suffer academically. Unfortunately, the warped sense of devaluing diverse groups has funneled its way down to the unprotected preschooler. Arresting preschoolers seems the next natural or unnatural state of progression for education systems. Perhaps this assertion is a slight exaggeration, but inequality in preschool is real, and it can be obliterated if we implement a system that has as its goal equality and excellence.

Feeling the effects of inequality in school is harmful enough; we cannot continue to operate in educational spaces that perpetuate punitive practices that continue to disadvantage marginalized groups. This book is about solutions, and uses wellness domains to help turn around the efforts of inequality that ruin the lives of many marginalized students. Teachers need more support and systems that will help them to become part of the social change that supports all students. Teacher support is required to produce the superior citizens we wish to see. Eight wellness domains work together with eight leadership competencies; the system infuses and addresses the needs of the whole child.

Chapter 10

The Depth of Wellness

Wellness encompasses a healthy body, a sound mind, and a tranquil spirit.
Laurette Gagnon Beaulieu

OBJECTIVES

- ✓ Understand how to be proactive in the classroom.
- ✓ Help teachers understand the difference between health and wellness.
- ✓ Clarify how a system of wellness improves academics.

School systems and education researchers will expound on the importance of students being afforded a wellness education; however, not many classrooms support or know how to implement a robust wellness program. Part of the reason for not implementing wellness education could be because some perceive wellness topics as topics that should be taught at home, or that wellness is not as important as content area subjects. If we examine educational goals in the 21st century, it becomes difficult to rationalize the exclusion of wellness education in the classroom. Explicit training should be on the implementation of wellness domains. All teachers should be instructed on the importance of including a wellness focus into their daily activities and instruction.

Health education is not wellness education. Health and wellness are terms that are often interchanged. However, health refers to being disease free, whereas wellness refers to the whole of what is needed to ensure health and well-being throughout life. If our goal is to create SCHOLARs, if our goal is to ensure that our SCHOLARs are leaders in the making, then we must address wellness. If we are to put our children first, we must address the whole child systematically.

For the reasons already mentioned, wellness must have a clear definition and a way to be incorporated easily into the daily landscape of school activities. In fact, Greenberg, (1985) distinguished between health and wellness, noting that health depends on knowing how to become well in order to ensure a complete health picture. In other words, health will be difficult to attain without a system that incorporates wellness. Wellness education is integral to the education system and important for our students. When we make a conscious effort to educate the whole child/student, we will produce SCHLOARs that are ready to take advantage of future college, workforce, and entrepreneur opportunities.

Myers, Sweeney and Witmer (2000) described wellness as "a choice and that each choice made toward wellness empowers an individual toward overall well-being" (p.258). Wellness researchers have considered the development of wellness as an evolving process of consciousness. Educators are in a position to help students to make positive choices in and out of school. Unlike punitive practices, which are considered negative, wellness education is positive and affirms the best in students. Corbin and Pangrazi (2001) developed a professional framework for educators:

1. Professional organizations should endorse a uniform definition of wellness.
2. Use a uniform definition to promote an understanding of wellness.
3. Programs of wellness must include more than activities and fitness.
4. Wellness can be a useful term that need not be avoided (p. 8).

With a wellness framework and a system in which to implement wellness domains, educators can be in the vanguard of producing the leaders we wish to see in the future. There are many definitions to wellness; I have identified eight wellness domains that are connected to leadership competencies. 360CL connects wellness, literacy, and leadership into a system that will run throughout the school year.

Quick Synopsis Work: Describe how wellness is connected to education and teaching.

Chapter 11

Four Components Of 360CL

If you can't describe what you are doing as a process, you don't know what you're doing.

W. Edwards Deming

OBJECTIVE

✓ Understanding the four concepts of 360CL

Components To Teach 360CL

Implementing 360CL as a parallel educational entity will require developing a common understanding of all of the components and methodologies. The goal and purpose of the system is to ensure that students are being taught in learning environments that support academic and personal success. Having the ability to thrive throughout life should be the reason for educating students. We want our children to be fully equipped to handle any challenges their lives may present. Four areas influence the system of 360CL. Cultural Leadership Mastery, Cognition Scale Mastery, Application Mastery, and Wellness Mastery comprise most of the system. It is important that stakeholders understand the purpose and importance of all four areas clearly.

1) Cultural Leadership Mastery (Diversity)

Connecting culture and leadership is a process, and over time, teacher mastery will provide the opportunity for marginalized student groups to thrive. When teachers understand how to incorporate 360CL into their instructional strategies, their cultural effectiveness will improve. Teachers will know how to connect diverse cultural contributions from their students' backgrounds into the culture of the classroom. Cultivating the intellectual properties of all students will help to create a positive and sustainable learning environment.

One exercise or discussion does not make a cultural leader; however, with participation and practice, the cultural leadership process will become second nature. Relax, make mistakes, and call an expert when needed. Ideas of perfection and stress will not help when making a paradigm shift.

2) Cognition Scale Mastery (Fluency and Reading)

Preschoolers are beginning to learn about process. Part of the process that we want them to participate in at the foundational level is acquisition of the skill of recognizing differences. We want our young SCHOLARs to observe all of the learning styles evident in their classroom. Preschool teachers want to have robust conversations about different types of learning styles while ensuring that students know that all types of learning styles are valuable. Teachers should seek to master the nuances of the Cognition Scale in order to feel confident enough to help students to know how perfect they are.

3) Application Mastery (Application)

Application mastery provides opportunities for students to apply what they are learning to real-life situations. Students should be encouraged to produce products and solve challenges. Producing products and solving challenges on a consistent and regular basis allows students to develop such vital skills as dreaming and solution visualization.

4) Wellness Implementation (Wellness)

Wellness in school systems includes a broad range of flexible activities that help students to balance what they learn in school with their future success. Social and communicative skills are practiced so that students have the opportunity to witness how their skills can influence and benefit their lives positively. Wellness domains will benefit students in and out of school, so they should be afforded the opportunity to learn and use the language of cultural leadership every day.

Chapter 12

Success Wellness and Listening

(Week 1 Action)

Constantly introduce positive skills needed for academic and personal development

OBJECTIVES

- ✓ Guide teachers to explore their beliefs about success wellness.
- ✓ Help teachers understand the connection between academics, listening and success wellness.
- ✓ Clarify the importance of listening and success wellness.

Success Wellness and Listening

First Week

The first week of preschooler 360CL will incorporate the first domain, success wellness, and the first competency, attitude.

Success Wellness and Listening

Teachers will explain the concept of success wellness and the connection to listening. Teachers will provide students with tools and practices that help to understand the process of listening. Teachers will explain the benefits students will gain from acquiring the skill of listening. Students often believe they already know how to listen, students must understand the difference between hearing and listening. We know that **hearing** is a physical ability and **listening** is a learned skill.

Listening Skills System

Listening is a system that has three parts.
1. Hearing the speaker.
2. Understanding what the speaker wants you to know.
3. Having the ability to use the information that the speaker has provided to make sound decisions or provide educated feedback.

Why Teach Your Preschooler Listening Skills?

1. Listening skills (if applied) will help your preschoolers to become master students.
2. Listening skills (if applied) will give preschoolers the skills to be productive working partners.
3. Listening skills (if applied) helps preschoolers resolve difficult communication challenges.
4. Listening skills (if applied) helps preschoolers to show support for others.
5. Listening skills (if applied) helps preschoolers to find understanding and meaning in what others are trying to say.

What Master Listeners Know

1. Master listeners know what is happening around them.
2. Master listeners know how to learn new things.
3. Master listeners know how to increase their chances of meeting and gaining new friends because as they listen, they are showing an interest in other people.

What Listening Masters Do

1. Master listeners always keep focused eye contact.
2. Master listeners sit still with their mouths closed.
3. Master listeners acknowledge the speaker by nodding.
4. Master listeners pay attention during lessons, let the teacher finish giving instructions, and raise their hands and ask for clarification.

Recognize Negative Listening Habits

1. Negative listeners believe they do not need to listen to some people because they have decided what others are going to say is stupid.
2. Negative listeners fidget or talk while someone else is talking.
3. Negative listeners get angry when someone else is talking.
4. Negative listeners lack the listening skills needed to listen when someone else is speaking.

Success Wellness and Listening

Riehle and Weiner (2013) attributed student success with high-impact activities. High-impact activities engage preschoolers in solving challenges. Success is the first word in the SCHOLAR acronym; therefore, preschoolers should begin to develop habits in their day that consist of activities that promote opportunities for them to feel successful. Purposeful activities allow preschoolers to engage in the purposeful tasks. High-impact activities for preschoolers will usher in the practice of student investment in real-world situations. When spoken, the language of success will begin to permeate the psyche of the preschooler. Teacher modeling helps students connect to their newly found knowledge.

Understanding success wellness involves developing a common language of success as well as identifying and linking success to the skill of listening. Success wellness when mastered should produce: (a) preschoolers that can organize and use what they have heard and can complete tasks; (b) preschoolers that can communicate what they must do to complete the tasks, and (c) preschoolers that finish the tasks with pride. Preschoolers will fall short of success skills if they do not master listening. Students should have the opportunity to delve more deeply into what success is and how it makes them feel. Preschoolers will have plenty of opportunities to practice their listening skills when they arrive to school, during transitions, before and after activities, in line, at lunch, and when it is time to go home.

Quick Synopsis Work: Write your own idea of a high impact listening activity.

Chapter 13

Social Wellness and Empathy

(Week 2 Action)

Peer etiquette skill development

OBJECTIVES

- ✓ Guide teachers to explore their beliefs about social wellness.
- ✓ Help teachers understand the connection between academics, empathy and social wellness.
- ✓ Clarify the importance of empathy and social wellness.

Social Wellness and Empathy

Second Week

The second week of preschooler 360CL will incorporate the second domain social wellness and the second competency, empathy.

Social Wellness and Empathy

Teachers will explain the concept of social wellness. Social wellness for preschoolers involves teaching about accepting differences in all students. Preschoolers will be involved in activities that teach about how to respect other students. Teaching empathy will allow students to know the importance of accepting who they are while accepting who other students are.

Empathy Skills Building

Empathy skill building will include using fairytales to help preschoolers understand how other people feel. Some feelings to discuss and help preschoolers explore empathy are:

1. Happiness
2. Disappointment
3. Anger
4. Excitement

Why Teach Your Preschooler Empathy?

1. Empathy skills (if applied) will help preschooler become aware of their feelings.
2. Empathy skills (if applied) will help preschoolers understand the feeling of others.
3. Empathy skills (if applied) will help preschoolers know they can help solve problems of others.

What Master Empaths Know

1. Master empaths know that listening is essential to get to know people.
2. Master empaths know not to feel sorry for people; instead they know to help people.

3. Master empaths know that it is fine to feel what others are feeling and saying is important.

What Empath Masters Do

1. Master empaths help.
2. Master empaths listen.
3. Master empaths find solutions to problems of others.

Recognize Negative Empathy Habits

1. Negative empaths are sympathetics.
2. Negative empaths appear to care and help others but they are only interested in their own needs.
3. Negative empaths do not listen to the needs of others.

Social Wellness and Empathy

Social wellness in preschool will mean providing preschoolers high impact activities that introduce preschoolers to empathy. Preschool teachers already help students play fairly with their peers, so the idea of explicitly using social games to help preschoolers understand the feelings of empathy will fit into the social games that are already in place (Howes & Matheson, 1992). Preschool social games help preschoolers get involved with the process of interactive play that teaches students to understand simple daily activities like taking turns while understanding that everybody will be afforded a turn. Patience will be part of the process of social wellness. Teachers will be cognizant of the effectiveness or ineffectiveness of the games preschoolers are participating in. Are the games yielding the play power or impact teachers are hoping for ? Are the games in need of restructuring? Do all of the teachers understand the theory and psychological methods of social games?

Anthony et al. (2005) offered suggestions about preschool behavior as it relates to a broad spectrum of social relationships; parental relationships, parental behavior as it relates to preschool behavior, and social competence and behavior problems. Although teachers cannot control home activities, teachers can invest in social games that help counteract possible negative behaviors preschoolers might witness at home. Social games help children develop the ability to positively interact with their peers; they also help children interact positively with their teachers. Teachers often blame the family lives of students as a reason children cannot thrive. Although family life is a part of the equation, our job is to find the part of social competence we can advance.

Quick Synopsis Work: Use your imagination and design an empathy activity using two or three of the following faces.

_____

_____

_____

_____

_____

_____

_____

Chapter 14

Value Wellness and Self-belief

(Week 3 Action)

Seeking meaning and purpose while developing core values

OBJECTIVES

- ✓ Guide teachers to explore their beliefs about value wellness.
- ✓ Help teachers understand the connection between academics, self-beliefs and value wellness.

Value Wellness and Self-Belief

Third Week

The third week of preschooler 360CL will incorporate the third domain, value wellness, and the third competency, self-belief.

Value Wellness and Self-Belief

Teachers will explain the concept of value wellness and to preschoolers. Preschool teachers will help students understand that value means doing no harm. Preschoolers will have an opportunity to participate in activities that support adding value to all lives.

Self-Belief Skill Building

Self-belief skill building will include using "I AM" words and activities to help preschoolers understand how they feel about who they are. Descriptive words will include terms such as:

1. Smart
2. Dumb
3. Beautiful
4. Lazy

Why Teach Your Preschooler Self-Belief Skills

1. Self-belief skills (if applied) will help preschooler become aware of their feelings.
2. Self-belief skills (if applied) will help preschoolers understand their thoughts.
3. Self-belief skills (if applied) will help preschoolers know they are unique.

What Master Self-Belief Preschoolers Know

1. Master self-belief preschoolers know they can change and improve ideas and behavior.
2. Master self-belief preschoolers know their self-beliefs have value.
4. Master self-belief preschoolers think positively about who they are.

What Master Self-Belief Students Do

1. Master self-belief preschoolers define who they are or wish to be.
2. Master self-belief preschoolers are motivated to learn the process of change.
3. Master self-belief preschoolers learn to feel good about choices they make.

Recognize Negative Self-Belief Habits

1. Negative self-belief habits promote self-doubt.
2. Negative self-belief habits cause students to act out negatively.
3. Negative self-belief habits create feelings of anger.

Value Wellness and Self-Belief

Value is the percentage we ascribe worth to others and ourselves. Schwartz (1994) identified ten motivational types of value: power, achievement, hedonism, stimulation, self-direction, universalism, tradition, conformity, security, and benevolence (p. 22). Teachers often struggle with motivating students; incorporating self-directed learning techniques in order to spark curiosity in preschoolers will help motivate preschooler's value in their learning. When preschoolers become curious, teachers can begin discussions and activities to help them delve deeper into their learning process; curiosity at playtime can be the impetus needed to connect activities with self-directed learning. Self-directed learning techniques have the possibility of helping preschoolers develop positive self-beliefs about their own process of learning. 360CL addresses and cultivates four motivational values: helping students value their own power, achievement, academic stimulation, and self-direction.

We want our preschoolers to know they have value. One way of encouraging self-value is to help preschoolers understand what self-beliefs are. Students will have the opportunity to discover some of the ideas they have about who they are and what they believe. The more opportunities afforded to students to help them compare who they are to a character in a story, or compare the actions of a character to an action they have taken they will begin to participate in the process of their own self-beliefs. The first step to the process of self-beliefs could begin by uncovering and building on a positive self-image. Teachers will be instrumental in asking "What do you think of……."; teachers will be able to talk about ideas of who they are as a teacher and how they had to work on habits they found not to benefit them. For example, teachers will help their students if students know that even their teachers have self-beliefs that could change. As students learn the process of incremental improvement, students will know and feel success and personal power.

Quick Synopsis Work: Use the space below to create a fun "I Am" Worksheet. Make sure you have fun creating the "I Am" pages for students to begin to discover their worth or value. The following words can be used as I am fillers.

I am smart.

sad.   helpful.

As a variation to I AM worksheets, students can make I AM necklaces to wear. They can read their statements throughout the day.

I am
smart.

Use this page to create an **I AM** worksheet or necklace.

Chapter 15

Cultural Wellness and Confidence

(Week 4 Action)

Developing cultural awareness to aid in personal growth and pride

OBJECTIVES

- ✓ Guide teachers to explore their beliefs about cultural wellness.
- ✓ Help teachers understand the connection between academics, confidence and cultural wellness.
- ✓ Clarify the importance of confidence and cultural wellness

Cultural Wellness and Confidence

Fourth Week

The fourth week of preschool 360CL will incorporate the fourth domain, cultural wellness, and the fourth competency, confidence.

Cultural Wellness and Confidence

Teachers will explain the concept of cultural wellness and the connection to confidence. Introducing preschoolers to cultural concepts will involve constantly demonstrating through visual representation, difference. Examples of difference can be found in all aspects of nature; people, animals, flowers, clouds, and trees. Examples of all sorts of differences in nature are plentiful and endless. Explanations of diversity will help students understand their own thoughts about who they are and how they think of others that are different.

Confidence Skills Building

Preschool teachers must provide opportunities and language that support the cultivation of confidence. Opportunities to build confidence could include providing real-life opportunities that allow preschoolers the chance to provide solutions to real life challenges to help build confidence.

Why Provide Your Preschooler Opportunities to build Confidence

1. Confidence skills (if applied) will help preschooler become aware that they can solve problems for other people.
2. Confidence skills (if applied) will help preschoolers understand that by helping others they will feel valued in their solution strategies.
3. Confidence skills (if applied) will help preschoolers know they are an important part of a community.

What Confident Students Know

1. Confident preschoolers know they feel good when they help others.
2. Confident preschoolers know they have talent.
3. Confident preschoolers know have the ability to change a situation if they try.

What Confident Masters Do

1. Master confident preschoolers help those that need help.
2. Master confident preschoolers feel good about helping others.
3. Master confident preschoolers begin to develop their identified skills.

Recognize Negative Confident Preschool Habits

1. Negative confident preschooler habits can promote insecurity.
2. Negative confident preschoolers can have anxieties.
3. Negative confident preschoolers show signs of timidity.

Cultural Wellness and Confidence

High impact preschool activities in cultural wellness involve a plethora of activities. Displaying examples of diversity in nature offers many opportunities to create a rich diverse learning environment. Academic and socioemotional goals include providing opportunities for students to learn how to accept difference. Teacher language is essential; teachers must feel comfortable talking about diversity as well as being able to implement diverse activities that are purposeful. Part of a rich cultural classroom experience involves the inclusion of students' lives. Deep engagement from students occurs when they feel they are part of the process. Brown (2004) offered recommendations for teachers that have as their goal a culturally rich classroom; the atmosphere should address students' cultural, ethnic, and cognitive needs.

Culturally effective teachers are aware of their biases and work to understand and use the background of students in order to enhance the teaching and learning experience. Culturally effective teachers have as their goal not the control of their students; instead they are interested in providing equitable education for all students. Teachers that lack cultural effectiveness often experience problems in the areas of behavior. Classroom management is the first essential component to create an environment in which students behave with a sense of leadership so that students begin to develop a sense of ownership in their learning. Students should be free of fear of unfair punishment so students can grow cognitively, culturally, socially, and emotionally. Teachers that utilize the following suggestions can help improve their cultural effectiveness:

1. Teachers should recognize their views and biases as they relate to their own cultural idea.
2. Teachers should be cognizant of diverse cultures and backgrounds of their students.
3. Teachers should be aware of the social or economic environment and any other barriers that have created difficulty for their students; access to and knowledge of resources is essential.
4. Teachers need the ability to reflect on personal teaching strategies and the skills to change what is not working.
5. Teachers need an open mind and commitment to developing a rich cultural classroom.
6. Teachers should know when it is time to call or reach out to a cultural expert.

Quick Synopsis Work: Describe a cultural effective teacher.

Chapter 16

Intellectual Wellness and Attitude

(Week 5 Action)

Open mind to new ideas while taking control of personal goal attainment

OBJECTIVES

- ✓ Guide teachers to explore the r beliefs about intellectual wellness.
- ✓ Help teachers understand the connection between academics, attitude and social wellness.
- ✓ Clarify the importance of attitude and intellectual wellness.

Intellectual Wellness and Attitude

Fifth Week

The fifth week of preschooler 360CL will incorporate the fifth domain, intellectual wellness, and the fifth competency, attitude.

Intellectual Wellness and Attitude

Teachers will explain the concept of intellectual wellness and the connection to attitudes. Teachers will teach preschoolers that there are a myriad of intellectual wellness styles; there are many ways students learn and no one way is the best way. Teachers will explain that all students learn differently and that as a teacher she/he will help students discover the best way they learn. Preschoolers will learn how to define parts of their intellectual wellness needed to be successful.

Attitude Skills Building

Attitude skill building is an important cultural leadership skill to attain. Preschool teachers must use their auditory skills to listen for language that supports great attitudes and language that supports bad attitudes. Plans should be in place to address language and actions that help improve negative attitudes and expand the concept of how an attitude can help you become a scholar.

Why Teach Your Preschooler about Attitudes?

1. Positive attitude skills (if applied) will help preschooler have more successful classroom experiences.
2. Positive attitude skills (if applied) will help preschoolers understand the feelings of other classmates.
3. Positive attitude skills (if applied) will help preschoolers work in harmony in the learning environment.

What Master Attitude Builders Know

1. Preschoolers with a master attitude know how to communicate what they need and want without a tantrum.
2. Preschoolers with a master attitude use their manners to speak respectfully to their teachers.

4. Preschoolers with a master attitude often believe it is their duty to help other students adjust their bad attitudes.

What Attitude Masters Do

1. Preschool attitude masters are cognizant of good feeling.
2. Preschool attitude masters help others adjust.
3. Preschool attitude masters feel they are part of the attitude solution team.

Recognizing Negative Attitudes

1. Negative attitudes can change positive dynamics of the classroom to negative dynamics.
2. Negative attitudes often produce negative speech and actions.
3. Negative attitudes in the classroom often break rules of behavior and are subject to discipline more than other students are.

Intellectual Wellness and Attitude

Examples of intellectual wellness occur in classrooms everyday and all day. Intellectual wellness can be detected with simple academic and nonacademic activities. Teachers that observe conversations students have during play can glean a multitude of intellectual data that can be used to help shape the intellectual profile of their preschoolers. Teachers will determine the level of intellectual skill of the preschoolers through collecting data; however, teachers must also be aware of the many types of intellectual abilities students will demonstrate. Teachers and parents should collect data that could support the type of intellectual intelligence the student appears to posses. Gardner and Hatch (1989) described the use and importance of using Gardner's list of intelligence. Although teachers are familiar with the work of Gardner, teachers often find it difficult to identify and incorporate all of the types of student intelligence while making sure lessons and standards are being administered. However, as there is more focus on differentiation it seems inconceivable that teachers will not follow Gardner's list of intelligence in order to identify and service the vast array of student intelligence. Teachers can and should be cognizant of at least eight different intelligence types as identified by Garner. The list includes:

1) Naturalist – students that are considered naturally smart
2) Logical-mathematical- students that are naturally good with numbers
3) Existential- students that are smart with matters of life
4) Interpersonal- students that are people smart
5) Musical- students that are gifted in music
6) Body-kinesthetic- students that have a propensity for the art of movement
7) Linguistic- students have a natural gift for language development
8) Intra-personal-students that are naturally smart and often engage in self-teaching
9) Spatial- students that are drawn to the arts

Although teachers are taught to refer to Garner's list of intelligence, teachers should not ignore any other types of intelligence they might identify or even discover.

Quick Synopsis Work: Describe a cultural effective teacher.

Chapter 17

Emotional Wellness and Discipline

(Week 6 Action)

Understand feelings and coping with stress

OBJECTIVES

- ✓ Guide teachers to explore their beliefs about emotional wellness.
- ✓ Help teachers understand the connection between academics, discipline and emotional wellness.
- ✓ Clarify the importance of discipline and emotional wellness.

Emotional Wellness and Discipline

Sixth Week

he sixth week of preschooler 360CL will incorporate the sixth domain emotional wellness and the sixth competency, discipline.

Emotional Wellness and Discipline

Teachers will explain the concept of emotional wellness and its connection to discipline. Teachers will provide activities that will afford the preschooler opportunities to reflect on choices they make. Emotions range from joy to anxiety; stable positive emotions are needed in order to help create habits like staying on task. Staying on task is part of discipline. When preschoolers do not learn how to handle their emotions, academic endeavors such as staying on task can be difficult for the preschooler to achieve. Mastering classroom discipline is a difficult process for some students; however, discipline is needed to help preschoolers learn how to follow classroom rules. Personal discipline is needed to help understand and control emotions. As preschoolers practice and engage in a range of their own emotions, they will develop an understanding of emotional wellness and discipline.

Discipline Skills Building

Discipline skill building activities help preschoolers learns how to change or improve their self-discipline. Self-discipline includes many skills; planning, awareness, action steps, and understanding consequences. Preschool teachers must be cognizant and observe patterns of behavior they witness with their students in order to understand how to shape activities that will improve self-discipline skills of their students.

Why Teach Your Preschooler Discipline?

1. Discipline skills (if applied) will help preschooler learn about consequences.
2. Discipline skills (if applied) will help preschoolers understand their actions.
3. Discipline skills (if applied) will help preschoolers know they can have control of their emotions.
4. Discipline skills (if applied) will help preschoolers use their new skills to improve their communication in and out of the classroom.

What Master Disciplinarians Know

1. Masters discipline preschoolers know they have consequences for their actions.

2. Master discipline preschoolers know how to self-regulate to improve their behavior.

4. Master discipline preschoolers will be persistent in their quest to improve behavior.

What Masters Disciplinarians Do

1. Master disciplinarians are aware.

2. Master disciplinarians are proactive.

3. Master disciplinarians often practice self-reflection.

Recognize Negative Discipline Habits

1. Negative discipline means to put off work until later.

2. Negative discipline promotes punitive experiences.

3. Negative classroom behavior disrupts the classroom learning environment and shows a lack of emotional discipline.

Emotional Wellness and Discipline

Emotional wellness is perhaps the most important wellness domain. When preschoolers do not develop positive emotional skills, their academic skills will suffer. Denham, Bassett, and Zinsser (2012) offered reasons why teachers must embrace and implement a strong foundation of emotional scaffolding in the classroom. Teachers play an important role in the socialization of preschoolers' emotional competence; it is imperative that preschoolers experience activities that promote the positive development of emotional wellness. Teachers along with parents and family experiences will be the architects of shaping the emotions of preschoolers; teachers must make sure preschoolers learn to listen, follow directions, play properly, and learn how to sit still. Regulating the emotions of preschoolers is a team effort; it can be difficult for many preschoolers to produce positive emotions because of life experiences. The earlier the detection of issues as they relate to emotions the easier it will be to help preschoolers. When preschoolers are able to handle their feelings, and are able to adjust their own feelings to benefit them, then preschoolers will be able to navigate productively both in academic pursuits and in personal communication.

Teachers helping preschoolers regulate their emotions might be challenging; however, if success of all students is the goal preschool teachers cannot sidestep this challenge. One of the major challenges for our preschoolers is the regulation of their newly formed social skill attainment. Success for all preschoolers might not be possible without a robust intervention that explicitly focuses on positively developing the emotions of the preschooler. If there is no intervention in place many preschoolers might risk being ill prepared for success in kindergarten and beyond. Teaching preschoolers how to regulate their emotions is a must if students are in training to be leaders. Teachers have a paucity of training in the area of teaching emotional regulations. Emotional regulation is a new field of interest for preschool researchers; emotions have been defined as a means of evaluating experience (Cole, Martin, & Dennis, 2004). Preschoolers that have challenges in the area of emotions may not be privy to the resources needed to improve their emotional circumstances. More importantly, if preschool teachers are not trained to recognize when emotional challenges exist they might mistake emotional difficulty for an unruly preschooler that needs constant punishment to help fix their bad behavior. When teachers understand that emotions can be regulated, more humane and positive solutions to preschool punishment can be implemented.

Quick Synopsis Work: Define and describe your idea of preschool emotional wellness.

Chapter 18

Physical Wellness and Failure

(Week 7 Action)

Maintain a healthy body both physically and mentally

OBJECTIVES

- ✓ Guide teachers to explore their beliefs about physical wellness.
- ✓ Help teachers understand the connection between academics, failure and physical wellness.
- ✓ Clarify the importance of failure and physical wellness.

Physical Wellness and Failure

Seventh Week

The seventh week of preschooler 360CL will incorporate the seventh domain physical wellness and the seventh competency, failure.

Physical Wellness and Failure

Teachers will explain the concept of physical wellness and its connection to failure. Teachers will provide the preschooler opportunities to participate in physical activities that address physical fitness and mental activities that address failure.

Physical Wellness and Failure Management

Preschools must determine if they have a physical wellness program or if they have time when preschoolers go out to play. Researchers that study the health of preschoolers are particularly concerned with preschool obesity. Considerable thought might be given to the adoption or creation of a physical wellness program. Part of any physical wellness program should include activities that teach about failure; failure is rarely emphasized or taught, however, the skill is needed to help preschoolers understand and manage failure.

Why Teach Physical Wellness with Failure Management

1. Physical skill development (if applied) will help preschooler know healthy food from unhealthy food.
2. Physical skills (if applied) will help preschoolers understand that movement is an important part of a healthy life.
3. Failure management skills (if applied) will help preschoolers know they can control their thoughts of disappointment.
4. Failure management skills (if applied) will help preschoolers understand that failures are mistakes that have not been fixed; remind preschoolers that all mistakes can be fixed.

How Mastering Failure Helps with Success

1. Preschoolers that master physical wellness know the importance of using exercise to stay healthy.

2. Preschoolers that master physical wellness know the importance of healthy eating to improve their overall well-being.

3. Preschoolers that master mental wellness know that failure can be used to get better academically.

4. Preschoolers that master mental wellness know that failure is helpful.

What Failure Teaches

1. Failure teaches pain and disappointment.

2. Failure can teach problem solving.

3. Failure can teach thriveability.

Recognize Failure is not Always Negative

1. Failure is thought of as negative because failure produces pain; however, if students learn how to use coping tools along with their failure they will learn that failure is natural and is not finite.

2. Failure is thought of as negative because the idea of failure is associated with not producing what is thought of as positive.

3. Failure is thought of as negative when students cannot see past the temporary setback.

Physical Wellness and Failure

Optimal health and wellness in adults begins way before adulthood. Physical habits and mental thoughts create states of wellness that reverberate throughout the lives of people. An increase in obesity, addictions, less play outside, poor eating habits, food deserts, and sedentary lifestyles, all contribute to poor physical and mental trajectories of our preschoolers. Burdette, Whitaker, and Daniels (2004) determined that not enough research has been done on the physical needs of preschoolers. Concerns are that those that educate preschoolers must be cognizant of all of the parameters necessary to produce the best SCHOLAR possible. If preschools follow the patterns of kindergarten and upper grades, children will see a decline in the time dedicated to physical activities. Academic pressure often supersedes time needed for physical activities.

Play is a natural state of being for children. The question is in how to maximize their play time to help preschoolers develop habits of health. Declining adolescent health has been contributed to the lack of habits that should be embedded and applied during earlier years of development. Pellegrini and Smith (1998) describe physical play as being more vital than we might have believed; they surmise that physical development improves cognitive performance and even play a part in the socialization processes necessary for social skill development. Teachers, parents, and researchers know that physical activities are essential to health and wellness, however; teachers, parents, and researchers must also place their efforts and concerns on all aspects of mental development. Imagination plays an important role in dealing with failure and mental development, not enough time is dedicated to teaching preschoolers how to use their imagination to solve mental challenges.

Imagination, according to Albert Einstein is more important than knowledge. Einstein's reasoning was that imagination allows for the birth of unseen and unimagined solutions. Imaginative preschoolers are curious, independent, and solution oriented. According to Lee (2005), creative thinking ability has a correlation to personality development. Lee believes that more preschool teachers should consider assessments used to evaluate preschooler potential. Understanding more about the powers of creativity in preschool is essential; creative thinking is part of being a leader.

Quick Synopsis Work:

Part I

List the physical activity types used in your preschool. Detail reasons you use the particular activity used; in other words, what is the expected outcome to the physical activity choices.

Part II

What opportunities and how much time is spent on expanding imagination. How are preschoolers using their imagination to solve problems?

_____

_____

_____

_____

_____

_____

_____

_____

_____

Chapter 19

Environmental Wellness and Awareness

(Week 8 Action)

Awareness and respect for our environment

OBJECTIVES

- ✓ Guide teachers to explore their beliefs about environmental wellness.
- ✓ Help teachers understand the connection between academics, awareness and environmental wellness.
- ✓ Clarify the importance of awareness and environmental wellness.

Environmental Wellness and Awareness

Eighth Week

The eighth week of preschooler 360CL will incorporate the eighth domain, environmental wellness and the eighth competency, awareness.

Environmental Wellness and Awareness

Teachers will explain the concept of environmental wellness and its connection to awareness. Teachers will provide the preschooler opportunities to participate in environmental activities that address environmental issues and activities that address awareness.

Environmental Wellness Skill Building

Environmental wellness for preschoolers starts with making students aware of environment issues. Teachers can help preschoolers develop environmental skills by providing real-life activities, discussing solutions with students, and discussing how students can help. Preschool awareness can begin with an issue as simple as recycling.

Why Teach Your Preschooler Environmental Wellness

1. Environmental skills (if applied) will help preschooler become aware of the importance of helping the environment stay healthy for future generations.
2. Environmental skills (if applied) will help preschoolers learn they can help with social issues.
3. Environmental skills (if applied) will help preschoolers know they can get involved with community concerns.

What Preschool Environmentalists Know and Do

1. Preschool environmentalists know they have the power to improve their environment.
2. Preschool environmentalists are in learning environments that makes them aware of social issues.
3. Preschool environmentalists use their imaginations to help solve environmental issues.

What Preschool Environmentalist Do

1. Preschool environmentalists are excited.
2. Preschool environmentalists learn how to improve their classroom or community.

3. Preschool environmentalists are involved with real-life solution activities.

Negative Environmentalists

1. Negative environmentalists are not concerned with environmental issues even when made aware of challenges in the classroom or community.

2. Negative environmentalists do not believe they can or should help the environment.

3. Negative environmentalists are not concerned with repurposing or recycling.

Environmental Wellness and Awareness

Teachers are concerned about making sure preschoolers connect with nature. Social scientists and education researchers have concerns for the lack of time children engage with nature; all children should be exposed to regular engagements with nature. It is never too early to get children involved with environmental issues. Smearsoll (2017) offered an exciting program that involves high school students that are teaching preschool children about environmental issues. This project-based program taught preschoolers about developing conservation skills.

Partnerships are the key to developing robust purposeful, engaging and exciting preschool projects that teach about the environment. Environmental partnerships might be the most abundant resource to obtain. Cities have local programs that are tied to parks and recreation groups. Preschool teachers can reach out to surrounding libraries, other schools, research state programs, and local community colleges. Environmental studies incorporate so many practices that lead to the development of leadership skills. Local and global environmental concerns are plentiful; there are many ways preschoolers will be able to be involved.

Quick Synopsis Work:

Part I

List as many environmental organizations your staff has knowledge of that support the local school system.

Part II

Take a few moments and discuss possible environmental issues that your preschoolers could get involved with. Start with a list of resources you presently have connections with and brainstorm on possible new partnerships you could establish that will enhance your environmental knowledge.

_____

_____

_____

_____

_____

_____

_____

_____

_____

_____

Chapter 20

New Preschool Ideas

Education is the most powerful weapon which you

can use to change the world.

Nelson Mandela

OBJECTIVES

- ✓ Understand how to implement a system of cultural leadership.
- ✓ Guide teachers to explore their beliefs.
- ✓ Help teachers understand the connection between academics and wellness.
- ✓ Clarify the importance of competencies and domains.

A New Idea for Preschool

This 2003 quote from Nelson Mandela could be written for today's social change leaders. Tainted water, poverty, gender, and wealth inequality, cultural indifference, climate change, food deserts, police brutality, health disparities, and undereducation are a partial list of the world environment that is being left for our students. Many government decisions are negatively impacting indigenous groups, and the lack of opportunities are increasing for many marginalized groups. Some researchers place the blame of the human condition on current and past leadership. Educators as social change leaders could be the answer to help students get prepared to change the trajectory of their lives. In order for students to effectively transform their environment they will have to be educated differently; their education will need to address the whole child, and an emphasis should be on personal leadership. Educating preschool children to become leaders and providing opportunities for them to practice their leadership skills will be essential if our goal is to produce leaders that will know how to change their world.

Social change is a process of changing or transforming what is considered by some to be social wrongs. Social change has the potential to solve present social inequities in a new creative way (Fiol, Harris, & House, 1999). Social change activities offer a spectrum of tools that are used to reshape existing social norms in some way (Seyranian & Bligh, 2008). As preschoolers evolve into adulthood, they will be confronted with a range of academic and social challenges, including racial inequality, poverty, mental health issues, and employment issues. Education systems will be responsible for providing the academic and social foundation needed for students to be able to maneuver through academic and social challenges. Preschool teachers can help their students to become prepared for their future challenges by incorporating a social change curriculum.

Curriculum should reflect what is in the environment of their students; however, teachers must have a clear definition of what a social change curriculum is and how to incorporate the concepts into practice. Foundational levels of language arts, science, and social studies should include the promotion of what it means to be human; teaching human skills such as empathy, listening, wellness, personal activism, and being aware of one's environment. When preschoolers are immersed in an environment that exposes them to a plethora of cultural experiences, children have a better chance of becoming productive and successful students. A great number of teachers begin their career with hope and optimism for the future of their students, only to find that after years of teaching they feel a sense of hopelessness and despair for the future of their students. Fullan (1993) posited that teachers would benefit the lives of their students if they combined moral purpose with skills needed to become change agents.

Social change curriculum does not supplant current academic responsibilities; the incorporation of a social change curriculum assists students in taking proactive roles in their own education. Teachers that are clear about their social change curriculum objectives are able to provide a learning environment that encourages social change thinking and skill development (Hackman, 2005). Social change curriculum involves many concepts of social change. A social change curriculum offers the opportunity for students to: (a) become aware of their individual needs; (b) become aware of societies basic needs, in order to understand how they fit into society; (c) develop the need to understand empathy in order to create skills for their personal leadership; (d) understand what is meant by personal dignity, and how their dignity practices benefit their lives and society; (e) and how becoming master readers helps them become successful students and citizens.

Remarkably, twenty-first century students are moving through their lives without the opportunity to explore differences in other groups of students. Unfortunately, without an educational social intervention students will not obtain the essential skills needed to create social change within their school or community. Core tenets of a social change curriculum for preschoolers include a focus on vocabulary acquisition, reading, understanding diversity, leadership, and health and wellness activities. A new idea for preschool curriculum includes providing children with a concrete foundation of literacy, and social activism in order to prepare them to improve the landscape of the world they will live in.

The concept of social change is a broad category; the program focus for teachers is specifically on preparing preschoolers to become leaders of social change. A Social change curriculum for preschoolers explicitly tackles issues of race, inequality, poverty, family and community. Education is the only system with a platform that can begin to dissolve the scourge of inequality in education, racial injustice, poverty, and dysfunctional communities. Education is one of the most powerful systems if it is provided with the proper tools to get the job done.

Chapter 21

Social Change For Power Teachers

Psychology cannot tell people how they ought to live their lives. It can however, provide them with the means for effecting personal and social change.

Albert Bandura, Social Learning Theory

Social Change Background

- ✓ Social change for POWER teachers
- ✓ Using a Social Change Curriculum
- ✓ Globalization and Social Change

Social Change for POWER Teachers

Proof Of Work Engagement and Retention (POWER) teachers actively engage in and deliberately show proof of stimulating activities that help to promote self-leadership in students. Preschool work can be structured with play; the play should have the purpose of student **E**ngagement; and academic and social-emotional **R**etention. Activities, lessons, and assessments are structured to ensure all students participate in an enriching learning environment. Learning environments should be culturally rich; content should have depth, students should be taught self-leadership through domains and competencies, and explicitly designed for the emerging preschool leader.

Power teachers are able to prove that all students have some unique quality that can be exposed and improved on. Preschool POWER teachers are dedicated to the success of all students; they recognize that the early foundation is important enough to engage in their own self assessment. Preschool teachers are the first teacher for some preschoolers or second teacher for others. Therefore, it is essential that preschool teachers explore and dissect their biases and ideas about who they believe their students are. A preschool teacher can be debilitating or nurturing. For the rest of their lives students will be affected by their early educational experiences. The early foundation must be succinct, meaningful, purposeful, and systematically structured in such a way that the system can follow students all the way through their educational journey. Leadership teaching starting in preschool means the POWER teacher is in the process of helping students facilitate their own self-management program. Preschool curriculums and daily activities are perfect opportunities to help students understand and develop skills to understand their own abilities, things they like, understand their emotions, help them make positive decisions, help them think critically, and learn how to master fluency in reading.

It is an exciting time to be a POWER preschool teacher; helping students grow and develop into leaders. Researcher findings offer evidence that early childhood education programming provides children with long- term benefits in cognitive and social-emotional skill development. The United States ranks 26th in preschool participation of four year olds and 24th in participation of three year olds. Countries outside the United States understand the importance of starting the education of a child at an early age. Early childhood education in the United States must begin with strong programming in order for children in the United States to begin their academic journeys with benefits that last for their entire lives.

Now more than ever, early childhood education is playing an important role in the lives of three and four year olds. Researchers have identified the importance of preschool education as it relates to cognitive development as well as developing affective skill development. For the aforementioned reasons, countries that have taken research data seriously have developed affordable and rich programs for preschoolers that help prepare children to be successful in kindergarten. Early child programs that focus on cognitive and affective development provide support for success in life after grade twelve. In recent years there has been an interest in curriculum and interventions that improve the social-emotional development of children.

Preschoolers' brain development makes them perfect vessels for a social change curriculum. During the early years, the brain develops in a way that allows for high levels of plasticity; this level is higher than in any other time in their lives. This rate of brain development causes some teachers to claim that preschoolers are like sponges. Teachers mean that children are sensitive, vulnerable and easily influenced by outside stimuli, and the internalization of their perception of who they are is malleable. Retention of new skills is also high; in this respect, choosing a curriculum that supports the whole child is essential. Therefore, it is imperative that the literacy environment possess a myriad of stimuli that help in the development of academic, social-emotional, and should begin the foundation for leadership development.

Using a Social Change Curriculum

Teachers play a critical role in meditating the social and academic curriculum. While acknowledging what students already know, teachers connect what they can to frameworks and models for thinking and organizing knowledge. Connections should be embedded within disciplines such as literacy, mathematics, social studies, and the sciences. Culturally responsive teachers realize that mastering academic knowledge involves understanding that content can provide multiple avenues to understand and access information. History offers a particular example. Students in the United States might study the expansion of the American West through the eyes of the pioneers and the politicians who supported the westward expansion. However, teachers might choose to present historical perspectives through the eyes of children, or through the eyes of the rich or poor, or through the perspective of minority populations. Teachers must consider how to approach curriculum as well as how to incorporate multiple visual representative tools in ways that curriculum becomes meaningful to all students; this is an important part of culturally responsive teaching.

Students need opportunities to build a capacity to handle new material, solve complex problems, and develop new skills by scaffolding their learning from what they already know through a series of increasingly complex experiences has the ability to shift the locus of control from the teacher to the learner. Curriculum should be anchored with historical community contributions, local connections can help bring subject matter to a realistic purposeful connection, connection that can be traced to the everyday lives of their students. Connecting student knowledge and skills to content knowledge must be a goal; however, if the content does not connect to historical, community, and global contribution of their children then we will not be in the process of moving education forward. Spend time on helping students learn the content. Use real life, authentic texts. Engage students in inquiry about things that matter to them.

Select curriculum that students can participate in; curriculum that is structured for learning but also reflect the way a student learns, what they already know, a clearly connected slant, and a purposeful and clear picture of what they can do with the knowledge. If you come from what some may consider a dominant group of people and you find that you are having more discipline infraction than teachers that share the same culture of their students then it might be time to consult a cultural expert. If you are teaching in a school where the majority of students do not look like you, and if you are frustrated from day to day then there is something you can do. If possible, imagine putting yourself in situations where you are not from the perceived dominant group, where you do not even speak the language because you just arrived and you do not know the norms and unspoken rules. Perhaps you can imagine that you remember coming to a foreign place with a parent or parents but you were taken away from them and are now with new parents in a new city. If you can imagine, recognize what that feels like. Do you sit and imagine with comfort or discomfort? Ask yourself these questions. What did I do to be effective or survive in that situation? What did others do that either helped or hindered my effectiveness? What would have helped me in that situation? Use the answers to these questions to help you structure how you interact with students.

Globalization and Social Change

Globalization and employer demands are moving education systems toward preparing students to obtain leadership and diversity skills needed to be successful in the workforce. Preparing teachers to prepare students will require teachers to acquire and apply culture and leadership competencies in their classrooms. Developing cultural teacher leaders (CTLs) is essential if the education goal is to positively shape the whole child; culture, a part of the whole child is often not included in the curriculum. Traditional curriculum provides cultural practices and history of the dominant cultural group; leaving out historical contributions of other cultures that are represented in the classroom. Culture, a part of the whole student cannot be separated from the student and is intricately woven into the communication, academic, and engagement processes in the classroom. Vision and mission statements define the importance of educating the whole child; most parts of the child are addressed; however, cultural inclusion is still mostly illusive in the majority of classroom in the United States.

Culture, or how to effectively include culture in the curriculum is too often left out of education models that claim to be the best at what works. Education systems often find it difficult to implement programs that explicitly help advance marginalized students. Cultural sensitivity has been identified as a systemic challenge for many education organizations. Training teachers to become sensitive to children that do not look like them or share socio-economical status requires additional teacher training; for many teachers the additional knowledge needed to be successful in a diverse classroom is not provided or minimally provided through teacher programs.

Teachers have their own cultures; information and beliefs from their culture develops mind- patterns, mind-patterns will dictate classroom conditions that reflect the teacher's culture. Teachers that struggle with cultural sensitivity in the classroom often use practices that are culturally mismatched and prove to be detrimental for marginalized students. Cultural teacher leadership helps teachers become culturally sensitive through a system of pedagogical changes. Preparing teachers to become culturally sensitive would require teachers to first become aware of the importance of cultural effectiveness training and then be willing to apply new skills needed to prepare all students for success in the 21st century.

Chapter 22

Rationale For Developing Cultural Leaders

I have accepted fear as part of life – specifically the fear of change

I have gone ahead despite the pounding in the heart

that says: turn back.

Erica Jong

Social Change Background

- ✓ Defining cultural reality
- ✓ A teacher archetype
- ✓ Cultural leadership and teacher pedagogy

Defining Cultural Reality

During the 1970's and 1980's school systems grappled with keeping social issues out of the classroom; issues of culture and diversity plague classrooms and caused many minority students academic hardships. When there is a cultural mismatch between teachers and students, communication and classroom participation often results in low achievement, higher expulsion rates, and a low level of literacy for marginalized students. Educators and researchers examined cultural mismatches as early as 1988; Villegas (1988) claimed that if the education system were honest in its assessment of student achievement they would acknowledge that all student success is based on the culture of the dominant group, putting minority students at an academic disadvantage. Teacher demographics have changed slowly and have not kept up with the demographics of their students. Teacher training on diversity has changed slowly causing generations of students to underperform in classroom settings. Feistritzer, Griffin, and Linnajarvi (2011) provided diversity teacher data over the years:

1986: 91% of teachers were White, 6% Black, and 2% Hispanic.
1990: 92% of teachers were White, 5% Black, 2% Hispanic, and 1% Other.
1996: 89% of teachers were White, 7% Black, 2% Hispanic, and 2% Other.
2005: 85% of teachers were White, 6% Black, 4% Hispanic, and 5% Other.
2011: 84% of teachers were White, 7% Black, 6% Hispanic, and 7% Other.
2015/2016: 80% of teachers were White, 7% Black, 9% Hispanic, and 2% Other (Taie & Goldring, 2017).

    Data provided is used to highlight the current picture of the racial diversity of educators in United State's classrooms. Diversity in public schools will steadily increase; however, teacher training in the area of cultural effectiveness has not kept pace with the needs of the students. Cultural mismatch will continue to create academic hardship for students of diverse backgrounds. Now is the time to implement methodologies, strategies, systems, and frameworks that will support teachers the teach students that don't look like them. It has been unfair to believe that minimally training teachers on cultural competence will result in cultural effectiveness.

Archetype of a Cultural Teacher Leader

Hirsch (1984) made an argument about the power of cultural literacy; asserting the idea that if academics defined and implemented the principles of cultural literacy in the early stages of education then adult illiteracy would improve. Cultural literacy made an impact in the 1980's causing many teachers and administrators to investigate the merits of implementing culture into the curriculum. The concept of cultural literacy has since moved from cultural literacy to multicultural, diversity, to culturally competency. Although it has been over fifteen years since Hirsch declared the importance of cultural literacy, for some educators the meaning, structure, and implementation of cultural in the classroom is still a vague concept. Decisive leadership and explicit curriculum goals would help new teachers as well as experienced teachers understand the importance of cultural in the classroom. Cultural teacher leaders (CLTs) are trained to infuse their curriculum with four conceptual areas; culture, leadership, social change, and 21st century skills.

To create a culturally rich classroom environment, teachers become skilled at infusing diverse support material into their content area. All culturally responsive classrooms begin their work using a universal culture of excellence (CE); the culture of excellence is a strategic foundation that has as an overarching goal of student excellence. When CTLs begin with CEs they begin to (a) implement appropriate discipline practices; (b) develop a more authentic communication with students and their families; (c) work through their own feelings in order to see the value in others; (d) take time to understand how outside influences are affecting behaviors in the classroom; and (e) use support materials to help ensure equity in academic practices while providing opportunities for student to develop personal and social leadership skills.

CTLs analyze and explore their own leadership practices. Reflective Teacher Leadership (RTL) is a structured process of self-reflection. Researchers often state teacher reflection as the most important component of being a CTL. Sparks-Langer and Colton (1991) posited that the cognitive area of teacher reflection focuses on how teachers use knowledge in their planning and decision making. Both culture and leadership impart influence on the lives of students; teacher influence is needed to articulate to students the importance of being social change agents.

Students as social change agents means that teachers must go beyond the core content to include skill building in areas that help students become stewards of their lives, school participation, community engagement, and global . Being aware of social structures that affect their lives is not enough to help prepare students for future

Teachers often loose site of the basic premise that they are in the business of serving students (García, 2011; Darling-Hammond, 2006). The realization that providing excellent academic services in order to serve our students creates a myriad of discussions about what type of services will be beneficial to help propel students to academic and personal success. Education researchers are now suggesting the implementation of 21st century skills in order to ensure a complete academic program is available for all students. The impetus for the implementation of 21st century skills comes from an over abundance of students that are leaving their education system ill prepared for the workforce or college. Competencies, according to Boyatzis (2008) will replace skill development in the 21st century. Twenty-first century competencies require action and intent; skills are based more on abilities and often are not explicitly linked to action oriented and intent.

Cultural Leadership and Teacher Pedagogy

Cultural competent teacher leaders are leaders that share the goal of empowering all of their students. Teaching pedagogy is student-centered and use real-life problem solving to improve students' critical thinking skills. Cultural teachers that lead incorporate reflective practices that help shape student learning outcomes. Teachers that strive to become culturally competent leaders acknowledge the importance of inclusion; they seek to expand cultural knowledge and work to expand and extend their knowledge in order to improves student participation, engagement, and functionality in the classroom.

Teachers that are cultural leaders use a framework that helps them ensure that their goals and objectives are fulfilled. Using a framework helps the teacher design culturally inclusive classrooms that support, student-centered engaging classrooms. CTLs framework consists of five concepts: (a) define your curriculum goals, (b) know your cultural group or groups you are targeting, (c) identify all resources, (d) seek funding resources, and (e) implement reflective assessments. One of the curriculum goals will be to reflect and include references that represent the student diversity in the classroom. However, for those classrooms that don't have a diverse population, the goal will be to expand the importance of diversity through explicitly teaching diversity through curriculum infusion. It will also be important to identify resources, often times resources are available in the form of approved community persons, organizations, or established online resources that share the same goal of improving diversity in the classroom. Acquiring additional funding resources will help teachers and schools bring diverse support programs; out-of-school mentors help to promote benefits of diversity and academic pursuits. Lastly, teacher reflection practices help improve the general culture of instruction.

CTLs are involved with specific activities that support the cultural framework; they embed cultural richness into mandated curriculum goals. One of the first activities the teacher will engage in is to create a depth in the curriculum. CTLs will self reflect by asking their team members or by personally reflecting if their instructional decisions are culturally responsible. Some questions that might help teachers reflect are:

1) Are my instructive tools I use in the classroom representative of marginalized groups?
2) Are the experiences of the cultural groups woven within the daily instruction of the classroom?
3) Are the instructional practices influenced by research-based theoretical methods of what works?

Resources are often a major concern for administrators and teachers. One economical way to ensure that diversity in the classroom is meaningful and inclusive is to gather information on the students' personal family history. By soliciting the background from students, teachers begin to learn more about their students while producing a product that can be used to define the culture of the school as well as connecting students to their curriculum. Researchers have long agreed that the more the students are connected to their academic work the more engaged students become. CTLs recognize that by actively collecting student data and using collected data in their classrooms they begin part of the process of implementing a robust learner-centered classroom.

Culture is a natural state of being and is involved with the shaping of children well before children are involved with the school system. Teachers will inherit a host of children that are different from them; not preparing teachers for success as it relates to being culturally competent will further jeopardize the future of many students that are presently marginalized in their present classroom and school environments. One of the first objectives will be in identifying what type of student product the education system will expect to produce. What is the role of culture in the process of student success? What present changes need to be thrown out and replaced with new academic structures that promote cultural inclusion? What common language and practices will facilitate the mission and vision of a culturally functioning school? Teachers in the 21st century must understand the importance of culture and how culture influences learning in the classroom. Cultural leadership teachers create learning environments that support success for all students from all cultures.

Chapter 23

Preparing Students For Success

Change will not come if we wait for some other person, or if we wait for some other time. We are the ones we've been waiting for.

We are the change that we seek.

Barack Obama

Social change Background

- ✓ Defining cultural reality
- ✓ Globalization and social change
- ✓ Clarify the importance of competencies and domains.

Domains and Competencies of Cultural Leadership

Cultural teacher leaders prepare students to become self-motivated learners that take the initiative to explore and promote their academic and personal destiny. Competencies are what students should be able to do or have the ability to accomplish. Cultural leadership competencies are arranged around the concept of personal leadership. Teacher expectation or intent is on having students become self-regulated. Cultural leadership is taught through a program design; the teaching design method focuses on the identified domains and competencies. One way teachers that teach students to become their own leaders accomplish this is by following a system. 360CL's framework includes eight domains and competencies.

In order for students to become productive and fully functional adults that are in control of making decisions that promote personal wellness, students need to develop more than just academic mastery. Researchers report that business leaders are in short supply of competent workers; colleges have determined that a great number of students are taking remedial classes because they are not ready to be successful in college. If 21st century skills do not include skill development in the areas of self-management, collaboration, and leadership then many students will not be prepared to function in the workforce, college, or as an entrepreneur.

Many teachers understand the importance of students receiving affective skill development; however, many teachers also feel overwhelmed and are not anxious to feel responsible for more responsibilities. Researchers are increasingly stressing the importance of providing students with preparation tools that can be useful in school and adulthood. CTLs use a domain conceptual model that consists of four domains. The four identified domains of this model includes; interpersonal, intrapersonal, leadership, and academic, workforce, and entrepreneurial (AWE) skills. Domains are broad identifiable concepts that are linked to a specific goal. The goal of CTLs is to provide all of the tools necessary for students to be successful. As the 21st century knowledge base is shifting from skill to competencies teachers need a framework that helps them incorporate domains and competencies into their curriculum.

Cultural Crafting for Classroom Teachers

Education should be responsible for improving the lives of its learners. For many marginalized students their education appears worthless. Culture or the misunderstanding of culture is one of the identified reasons many student subgroups are failing. Education and culture are intimately connected. Researchers have acknowledged that education should connect student heritages to their curriculum. Culture is responsible for how students adapt to their school and personal environments; education systems are expected to be part of the process of helping cultivate the socialization process of students. Education systems should inform students about the importance of their culture and how culture is integrally connected to student curriculum. Education should help students develop attributes that teach tolerance. In this way, education helps to develop the personality of their students. Education systems have the unique structure that can bridge the cultural gap by implementing curriculum and programs that support diverse cultures.

Education curriculum should treat the beauty in human culture as part of the daily curriculum. Twenty-first century teachers are expected to become curriculum construction-agents; their job is to craft cultural norms into their daily activities. Curriculum crafters must have an understanding of inter-cultural curriculum structure. Inter-cultural curriculum activities should provide the opportunity for students to develop an understanding of a myriad of cultures. Inter-cultural education helps students understand how people can have both differences and similarities and still exist harmoniously in society. Cultural crafters use old cultural stereotypes and experiences and reconstruct new academic experiences in order to produce new academic innovations.

Teaching in the 21st Century

Teachers in the twenty-first century are teaching with many pressures. New mandates require teachers to learn, shift, and implement new academic requirements while accountability pressures mount. Colleges, workforce, and entrepreneurs require students to have new skills that stretch beyond reading and writing. Colleges are offering more remedial classes in order to begin preparing students to be successful. Workforce developers acknowledge they are finding it difficult to acquire the talent they need to fulfill jobs. Budding entrepreneurs will need more than excitement to become successful; many lack the mathematical, communication, or writing skills needed to become successful.

Education researchers and data resources confirm that many subgroups in the education system are not achieving the success many of their peers are experiencing. Increasing diversity training for teachers will help improve the achievement gap of struggling subgroups. Will rigor be the answer? If yes, what type of rigor? Is the academic issue with the testing process? Is principal leadership the problem? Are parents doing their part? What part does curriculum play in student success? Do teachers really know how to be culturally effective? Perhaps we should define what teaching in the 21st century is in order to determine what teachers should do to ensure more student success.

As stated earlier, ART is needed for 21st century teachers to become crafters of cultural competency in the classroom. ART concepts begins with awareness; awareness should lead to questions. Reflection should lead to actions. Transformation should lead to changes in thought or practices.

Why Craft Culture into the Curriculum?

Education is an essential part of our social system and is responsible for shaping the thought processes of their students. Monocultural classrooms and curriculums have permeated the education systems for centuries. Traditional education models have overwhelmingly supported the social-emotional needs of students from the dominant culture. Therefore, the values, historic accomplishments, and instructional models have systematically perpetuated goals and the uplifting of the original education designers. Textbooks, pedagogical strategies, and visual representations consistently promote the dominant culture; these particular practices help shape how marginalized students view and participate in the education system. Education should be the vehicle that begins to correct the academic and systematic inequities; monocultural designs and practices should be viewed as an education disease that continues to harm students outside of the dominant culture. Educational changes provide the best way to bridge the cultural imbalance through the reconstruction of curriculum, strategic practices, textbook choices, and programs throughout the academic system.

Defining Cultural Crafting

Cultural curriculum crafters cannot assume there is one culture, a monoculture, or one type of culture that all of the students will work from and through. Misunderstanding of the importance of culture produces many classroom infractions. Daily academic activities of students impact how they view and experience their curriculum. The more we can engage students to be excited about how they learn and interact with what is being presented; the quicker teachers will see an improvement in in discipline.

Cultural Crafting Curriculum through the School System

Teaching is not often thought of as a craft. Crafting is often associated with making products such as soap, pillows, beer, or specialty chocolates. Merriam-Webster (2018), defines craft as a skill in planning, making or executing. Teachers that promote excellence in the 21st century should be engaged in planning, and executing required academic mandates. Successful cultural crafting teachers use academic mandates and then fashion and mold the information into a product that supports diversity.

Cultural Effectiveness

We have gleaned that eighty percent of teachers are white, a decrease from 82 percent in 2012. Nine percent of teachers are Hispanic, up from 8 percent previously. America's demographics are changing. The teaching pool will or should be changing to reflect the student body. The United States has seen a dramatic rise in the Hispanic population. Even so, the teaching force has not kept pace. About 7 percent of teachers are black and 2 percent are Asian. Those percentages have not changed since 2012. Although educators understand their student population is quickly becoming more diverse, teacher preparation has not kept pace in their efforts to prepare new teachers or provide all teachers with tools they need to be effective cultural teachers. More and different types of training or professional development must take place to preparing the teaching workforce to teach students that do not look like them or come from the cultural background of the teacher. Teachers cannot change their own backgrounds; but quite often their backgrounds or the lack of understanding of their students' backgrounds create friction. For example, African American children are expelled at higher rates than their counterparts; reasons for this is caused by problems in communication, understanding and teacher preparation.

21st Century Classroom Cultures

There will be a spectrum of cultures in the classrooms of today. If we are in the process of developing our preschoolers to become leaders, we will need to understand how we can implement systems that address cultures that will be involved in our education system. The following is a partial list of the different types of cultures teachers might experience in their classrooms.

1. Culture of Excellence
2. Culture of Race
3. Culture of Ethnicity
4. Culture of Hope
5. Culture of Success Language
6. Culture of Economics
7. Culture of LGBTQ
8. Culture of Gender

Chapter 24

360CL, Holism, Scholar, Process-Based Learning, Performance-Based Learning and Real-World Application

Social Change Background

- ✓ 360CL
- ✓ Holism
- ✓ School assessments
- ✓ Performance-based

360CL

360CL is a leadership system that was developed to ensure that all students have a better chance to be successful in their academic and personal lives. The system is beneficial for regular classrooms, gifted classrooms, and special education classrooms. The world needs more leaders. 360 addresses all aspects of what makes a well-educated child. 360CL was created to help develop and advance student independent learning styles, critical thinking, real-life applicable practices, and student engagement. 360CL also helps teachers become culturally effective in their classrooms.

How Does 360CL Work?

360CL has eight domain and eight competencies; basic background on what the domains and competencies are has already been presented. Each domain has a corresponding competency. Each week one domain and one competency will have either a classroom or school focus. For example, the first week's focus will be on the success wellness domain, and the accompanying competency will be listening. Teachers will begin the first week providing background about what success means and why it is important; they will do the same with explaining how listening is important. Teachers will also provide background for what makes a master listener. Students will be provided opportunities to practice listening, and will be engaged with discussions about success. Each week a new domain and competency will be introduced, at the end of the eight weeks an application should be designed to help preschoolers connect their new leadership skills to their academic activities and play.

Holism

Education holism defined in the system is a philosophical approach that considers and addresses the importance of the whole child. Holistic education operates using many components to assure that all parts of the child is addressed. Development means making sure preschoolers are learning about the type of learner they are. Weekly teacher assessments are used to help develop a learning profile of the preschooler; information gathered provides the teacher with essential academic and personal data. Holism as part of the system uses a mix of theories, methodologies, philosophies, competencies, domains, and assessments to ensure that all students will work in a learning environment of excellence.

Scholar Assessments

SCHOLAR assessments are used at the end of the 360CL week. SCHOLAR assessments are designed to be time and user friendly. Assessments will provide data that will be used to improve the performance of the preschooler, as well as providing teachers with vital data. An example of a SCHOLOAR assessment will be provided. Teachers might design their own assessment tool that will explicitly be used to track the progress of the SCHOLAR.

Process-Based Teaching

Process-based teaching for preschoolers is more concerned with making sure preschoolers develop habits and practices that produce excellence. For example, when preschoolers begin reading we want to listen for fluency, make sure their writing is foundationally sound, make sure they are using manners, are being polite, are mastering competencies from the system, and are making academic and social progress. Preschool teachers that are engaged in process-based teaching will use assessments as a tool to adjust teaching practices. Data will also be used as a communicative tool used to help communicate with parents. Process-based learning for preschoolers provides a variety of opportunities for preschoolers to develop skill mastery.

Performance-Based

Once preschoolers are engaged with the process of learning, they should begin to understand the purpose for learning. In other words, preschoolers should know that literacy practices are connected to application. Performance-based learning connects literacy to real-world applications. Preschoolers should be guided into discovering how to use the information gained from their lessons to solve some type of challenge, or to create a product with the information. Preschoolers should master processes in order to be in position to use their knowledge while connecting their processes to performance.

Chapter 25

Connecting Excellence In Teaching With Leadership

Social change Background

- ✓ Excellence in Teaching
- ✓ Supporting Material
- ✓ Marginalization of Students
- ✓ Cultural Reflection

Excellence in Teaching

360CL makes the assertion that teaching and learning takes place when there is a healthy robust academic system in place, a system that all teachers know, and are comfortable using. In order for teachers to understand what type of system they are working with, they need to recognize what a good and bad education system looks like. From this point on systems are referenced as either being ill or well. Ill academic systems operate with educational parts and pieces, however, the parts and pieces do not necessarily work in concert. For example, assessments might not align with the goals of the mission or vision of the school. Student outcomes might not be clear, activities might align more with busy work, and assessments might not help the student. A wellness academic system ensures that assessments align with learning outcomes; activities align with learning outcomes, and the goals of identified work works to improve student growth. Wellness systems are integrated. Project-based teaching works well with incorporating the needs of all students.

Preschools today that are interested in improving their rankings should operate with an academic system that incorporates a curriculum that addresses cultural, social-emotional issues, along with academic mandates, pre and post assessments, child screenings should be in place, the learning environment should have aspects of being interactive and the learning environment enticing. Systems that do not operate with an integrated system can be identified because there is not a clearly defined integration of research-based methods, there is usually a paucity of teacher training, low pay, and little support for teachers. Excellence in teaching requires thought, practice, and reflection. Equally important is the way instruction is administered.

Everybody in the classroom has the potential to teach something to someone. A successful classroom will be an environment that preschoolers know they can express their ideas and concerns openly. This will help the preschooler understand how they can become successful. Teachers must consistently communicate high expectations. Students will learn how to ask questions, connect content to their own lives, write to learn, read broadly, build mental models, test hypothesis, and make time to build relationships. Excellence in teaching means teachers will help facilitate self-directed practices that help students learn how they learn, while helping to provide all the resources, opportunities and practices.

Supporting Material

Building cultural competent classrooms and schools means going beyond concepts; creative actions are needed to go beyond curriculum and should include culturally rich:

- ☐ Books

- ☐ Videos

- ☐ Community Representatives

- ☐ Cultural Wall Images

- ☐ Presentations that Reflect Student Population

- ☐ Cultural Leadership Programs

Recognizing Culture and the Marginalization of Students

Cultural influences do not stop in the home; school learning environments also provide psychological influences as it relates to culture. When students do not connect who they are to their classroom experiences, they are less likely to connect or relate to lessons being taught. Students may begin a process of disengagement; results of the disengagement may not appear until middle school. Validating students' cultures requires using frameworks and strategies that target the identified population (Quintana, et al., 2006).

Practicing cultural exclusion in the classroom promotes the marginalization of many students that are different from the culture of their teachers. Many education system designs are presently operating with the methodologies and theories of the 20th century. In order to increase student success, education systems must move into practices that support 21st century methodologies and theories. Marginalized preschoolers begin their journey academically and mentally unstable and without an intervention, the state of instability will follow them throughout subsequent grades. Harbour and Ebie (2011) provide research that details the college life of marginalized students that enter community college; they report that marginalized students are not as prepared as their peers in the area of socialization, academically, or culturally.

Culture is involved with the shaping of children well before children are involved with the school system. Gay (2010) writes that students of color consistently are achieving at low levels at all levels and in all education systems. Teachers will inherit a host of children that are different from them; not preparing teachers to be successful as it relates to being culturally effective will further jeopardize the future of many marginalized students. Sleeter (2012) presents the argument that many teachers want to include more cultural elements in their daily activities but the pressures of standardized testing outweigh the acknowledged needs of their students. What is the role of culture in the process of student success? What classroom activities need to be discarded and replaced with new academic structures that promote cultural inclusion? What common language and practices will facilitate the mission and vision of a culturally functioning school? Teachers in the 21st century must understand the importance of culture, and understand how culture influences learning in the classroom. Cultural leadership teachers create learning environments that support success for all students no matter their cultural background.

A Cultural Framework

Culturally effective teachers use frameworks that help maintain their goals and objectives. Using a framework helps the teacher design culturally inclusive classrooms that support, student-centered classrooms. Culturally effective teachers also use systems. Below is a recap of what is needed to provide a culturally rich learning environment. Culturally effective teachers:

1. Define cultural curriculum goals.
2. Know cultural group or groups being targeted.
3. Identify all resources.
4. Seek funding resources.
5. Implement a reflective assessment process.

The first component defines cultural goals that include determining what strategies could be used to provide historical cultural connections into the daily activities. The second component helps the teacher recognize the diversity in the classroom while trying to gain personal and community knowledge about the cultural group. Gaining cultural backgrounds will help the teacher gain incremental knowledge about the diversity of students in the classroom. The third component focuses on identifying resources; resources go beyond monetary resources; resources could include community volunteers such as librarians, and business people. The fourth component could include grants that could be used to inspire outside experts to reinforce cultural connections. The last component involves developing a system of self-reflection.

Cultural Reflections in Teacher Practices

Culturally effective teachers develop reflective practices that help inform them about their professional teaching practices. Reflective practices help create a personal knowledge base tool that is used to help teachers become an effective teacher leader (Loughran, 2002). Some questions that help teachers reflect are:

1. Are my instructional tools used in the classroom representative of marginalized groups?
2. Are the experiences of the cultural groups woven within the daily instruction of the classroom?

3. Are the instructional practices influenced by research-based theoretical methods of what works?
4. Have my new strategies proven to be effective?
5. What activities have proven to be beneficial for certain students?

Teacher beliefs about teaching are constantly shaped and reshaped; transformation through reflective experiences helps develop teacher leadership skills (Walkington (2005). As teachers become aware of how their beliefs and pedagogical practices shape their classroom, and if they are willing to make changes, then their teaching practices will elevate the productivity of the classroom. Teachers often find awareness and changing their beliefs difficult. However, reflective practices are one of the most powerful tools new and experienced teachers have to improve their professional practices, while improving the lives of their students.

Challenges with Incorporating Cultural Leadership

Over the past two decades, educators have struggled with shaping content and pedagogy that helps all students thrive academically. Teacher leadership will not benefit students if administrators attempt to force change through stringent mandates (Smylie and Denny (1990). Teachers have their own teaching styles, idiosyncrasies, and beliefs. There is no one size that fits all when it comes to training teachers to become leaders; teacher leadership has many areas to be involved in and explore.

A global movement suggests that a new model of teaching is needed in order to prepare students for 21st century personal and academic success. A plethora of literature is available that supports the benefits of incorporating practices that help more students become successful; however, data that were collected also highlight the challenges that are present in teacher thoughts and practices that do not benefit success for all students. Researchers have identified three areas that could impede the implementation of cultural leadership practices in the classroom, they are: (1) teacher motivation for the implementation of a new model of teaching, (2) specific competencies and domains needed for teachers to become effective educational leaders in the twenty-first century are vaguely defined; and (3) the content, methodology, and pedagogy required to implement those efficacies are not taught or minimally provided in teacher training. Teachers that emerge as leaders for all of their children have a strong sense of purpose, reflect often, focus on student improvement and are driven by action (Lambert, (2003).

Cultural teacher leaders play a large role in shaping the workforce, college preparedness, and entrepreneurial skill development. Without specifying the type of leadership that is required for teachers to prepare all students, many students will be ill prepared for academic or personal success. York-Barr and Duke (2004) examines teacher leadership as part of the foundation that prepares teachers for expertise by increasing their depth of teacher skills and quality of teaching.

Researchers have identified and offered reasons for transforming teaching content and pedagogy in order to prepare teachers to help students meet a variety of academic and personal needs. Many disenfranchised youth are funneled into the prison pipeline system, dropout rates are increasing, students are not prepared for their futures, and more students are not identifying education as relevant. Students will learn aspects of leadership through actions and examples of the leadership they see through teacher and principal examples. Employers report worker shortages, while the pools of workers are often under-qualified. Many education practices do not align with skills and competencies needed for the workforce, higher education, or being an entrepreneur. Administrators, teachers, and parents have expressed concern about student preparedness as it relates to twenty-first century personal and academic mandates. In question are the level of critical thinking skills, level of imagination, and collaborative and communicative skills they will need to maneuver successfully in their futures. Revisioning our idea of a preschooler is the first step needed to begin a new process of preschooler education.

When to Call an Expert

Preschool teachers begin their careers with excitement and an eagerness to help their preschoolers succeed. However, there might come a time when the teacher realizes they are not witnessing positive behavior or academic success for all students. Upon reflection, the teacher might conclude that their learning environment is not providing the necessary essentials needed to promote academic and personal growth for some of their students.

All student groups will have a segment that will struggle with academic or behavior challenges. The way a teacher reacts to the challenge of student stress will have profound consequences for the student if the teacher's actions produce more stress for the student. Added student stress will usually produce more of the challenging behavior the teacher wishes to eradicate. All schools have corrective procedures that are in place to help students succeed. Part of the corrective or discipline protocol will require the teacher to collect data on the student in order to develop a plan of action to help the student improve. Another aspect of the plan to help the student will include reaching out to a parent or guardian in order to help resolve classroom issues. When the teacher has followed all steps in the improvement program, the last step will be to arrange a meeting with the head of the school. When meeting with the head of the school proves to be unfruitful, it might be time to be creative about finding alternative solutions. This might be the time to incorporate the services of an approved expert. Reaching out to an expert is part of a process to help stave off a punitive punishment or an expulsion.

Community experts and resources can be partners that help students, teachers, and schools with their vision and mission goals. No two students will need the same exact resources. Preschool teachers, administrators, and parent groups should create a list of resources and cultivate relationships that will help teachers and schools help their students. Teaching in the twenty-first century is a community affair. The days of handling difficult classroom situations totally inside the school may prove not to be the best model. Teachers and administrators might consider reaching out to community organizations that could be part of a solution team before the school needs the outreach help. Community experts come in the form of council people, businesses, grandparents, police persons, fire persons, community chefs, mental help organizations or counselors. Teachers should never feel they do not have adequate support; if the teacher feels added stress and frustration, the classroom environment will suffer.

Name_____

Date_____

SCHOLAR Assessment

Use the scale to assess student progress; 1 being the least and 5 being the greatest.

- [ ] **S**uccess with lesson   1   2   3   4   5
- [ ] **C**hoosing participation   1   2   3   4   5
- [ ] **H**abit development   1   2   3   4   5
- [ ] **R**eading fluency   1   2   3   4   5
- [ ] **S**ite words   1   2   3   4   5
- [ ] **O**wnership   1   2   3   4   5

How has your teaching lead to advanced readiness?

Weekly Cultural Leadership Focus

Week 1 Success Wellness	Week 1 Competency Listening
Week 2 Social Wellness	Week 2 Competency Empathy
Week 3 Value Wellness	Week 3 Competency Self-Belief
Week 4 Cultural Wellness	Week 4 Competency Confidence
Week 5 Intellectual Wellness	Week 5 Competency Attitude
Week 6 Emotional Wellness	Week 6 Competency Discipline
Week 7 Physical Wellness	Week 7 Competency Failure
Week 8 Environmental Wellness	Week 8 Competency Awareness

Repeat the cycle of eight three times. This will take the entire year. Teachers will use what they are already teaching. The system will run parallel to whatever is being taught.

Chapter 26

Teaching Leadership Versus Punitive Reactionary Actions

Social Change Background

✓ Stopping Punitive Expulsion.

Stop Punitive Expulsions

The book began with a question. Should we get prepared to accept the arresting of preschoolers or should we change the punitive practices that now exist in preschool while using a leadership model? After reviewing the cultural leadership system proposed in this book, I hope consideration will be given to engaging in conversations about punitive practices that might exist in your school. Preschoolers' potential for greatness is so exciting. However excited we are about our preschoolers, we must be equally appalled at the findings of researchers that educate us about four and five year old preschoolers' expulsion rates. We must be repulsed by the expulsion rates that preschool African American and Hispanic boys and girls are experiencing. Repulsion is only the first step; we must be proactive in our actions to improve the lives of all students.

Teachers must be cognizant of their beliefs and ideas that relate to children that do not look like them or share many of their cultural norms. Presently, some teachers seek first to punish and second to understand; if they seek to understand at all. Preschoolers cannot properly defend themselves; many preschoolers are trying to participate as best they can; however, some learning environments leave them emotionally and socially scarred. When this happens, their academic future is in jeopardy; before the preschooler starts, they will be behind.

All children have rich historical backgrounds; regrettably, many education systems are still teaching children as if there is primarily one right culture, excluding all other cultures have become the norm. Marginalized students are afforded cultural recognitions that include the celebration of Cinco de Mayo, Martin Luther King Day, and possibly some activities during Black History month; this paucity of inclusion is an indication that more teacher preparation is needed to improve the academic lives of their students. Marginalization can be pervasive and the devaluing aspect of it helps to promote expulsion practices.

Cultural knowledge and knowing what to do with the knowledge is needed to help teachers know how to improve punitive actions that exist in too many classrooms. Using a system steeped in culture, leadership, creativity, application, understanding, inclusiveness, celebration, wellness, theory, methodology, research and competencies will move school systems to education excellence for all students. A cultural leadership system will also address excessive punitive practices in a positive way.

We need to teach leadership now and as early as preschool. Our children must be able to know how to think, collaborate, be able to self-manage, understand that poverty is not an option, celebrate differences in people, and embrace the idea of well-being. The system of cultural leadership was designed to make teaching leadership easy. Conversations should begin around the subject of educational excellence and leadership in preschool. Preschool POWER teachers should be on the forefront of showing education communities how to become education social change agents. Together we can change the landscape, minds, actions, and negative trajectories that plague marginalized students, while intervening with the practice of excessive expulsions.

Our Final Preschool Product

Using a common language to define the idea of a preschool leader helps stakeholders know the specific goal a cultural leadership system hopes to accomplish; and that goal is to create leaders. We need to establish what we mean by preschooler. What's in the name PRESCHOOLER? There needs to be a concrete picture or identity of what we believe a preschooler is. We know that a preschooler is a little person full of promise and curiosity. If we read the acronym below and determine that the system used produced a preschool leader, then we will know we have prepared the whole child for kindergarten. We will gauge our little leaders based on the following description of a preschooler. A preschooler is a:

Preschooler

Ready for an

Engaging kindergarten

Education - a

Scholar ready for social

Change activities where

Healthy habits provide for more

Ownership development and

Opportunities to

Learn from a myriad of

Environments while being

Reading ready and able to take on a new kindergarten adventure.

When preschool teachers accomplish all of the above we will know we are participating in a cultural leadership program that is part of the solution.

References

Anthony, L. G., Anthony, B. J., Glanville, D. N., Naiman, D. Q., Waanders, C., & Shaffer, S. (2005). The relationships between parenting stress, parenting behaviour and preschoolers' social competence and behaviour problems in the classroom. *Infant and Child Development, 14*(2), 133-154.

Boyatzis, R. E. (2008). Competencies in the 21st century. *Journal of Management Development, 27*(1), 5-12.

Brown, D. F. (2004). Urban teachers' professed classroom management strategies: Reflections of culturally responsive teaching. *Urban Education, 39*(3), 266-289.

Burdette, H. L., Whitaker, R. C., & Daniels, S. R. (2004). Parental report of outdoor playtime as a measure of physical activity in preschool-aged children. *Archives of Pediatrics & Adolescent Medicine, 158*(4), 353-357.

Cole, P. M., Martin, S. E., & Dennis, T. A. (2004). Emotion regulation as a scientific construct: Methodological challenges and directions for child development research. *Child Development, 75*(2), 317-333.

Conley, D. T., & French, E. M. (2014). Student ownership of learning as a key component of college readiness. *American Behavioral Scientist, 58*(8), 1018-1034.

Corbin, C. B., & Pangrazi, R. P. (2001). Toward a uniform definition of wellness: A commentary. *President's council on physical fitness and sports research digest.* President's Council on Physical Fitness and Sports Research Digest, 3 (15), 1-8.

Covey, S. R. (2013). *The 7 habits of highly effective people: Powerful lessons in personal change.* New York: Simon and Schuster.

Craft.2018.In Merriam-Webster.com. Retrieved April 22, from http://www. merriam-webser.com/dictionary/craft

Darling-Hammond, L. (2006). Constructing 21st-century teacher education. *Journal of Teacher Education, 57*(3), 300-314.

Dalsgaard, S., & Otto, T. (2016). value, transvaluation and globalization. *eTropic: electronic Journal of Studies in the Tropics, 13*(2), 1-6.

Denham, S. A., Bassett, H. H., & Zinsser, K. (2012). Early childhood teachers as socializers of young children's emotional competence. *Early Childhood Education Journal, 40*(3), 137-143.

Feistritzer, C. E., Griffin, S., & Linnajarvi, A. (2011). *Profile of teachers in the US, 2011.* Washington, DC: National Center for Education Information.

Fiol, C. M., Harris, D., & House, R. (1999). Charismatic leadership: Strategies for effecting social change. *Leadership Quarterly, 10*(3), 449-482.

Fullan, M. G. (1993). Why teachers must become change agents. *Educational Leadership, 50,* 12-17.

García, O. (2011). *Bilingual education in the 21st century: A global perspective.* New York: John Wiley & Sons.

Gardner, H., & Hatch, T. (1989). Educational implications of the theory of multiple intelligences. *Educational Researcher, 18*(8), 4-10.

Garrett, J. L. (2006). Educating the whole child. *Kappa Delta Pi Record, 42*(4), 154-155.

Gay, G. (2010). *Culturally responsive teaching: Theory, research, and practice.* Teachers College Press.

Greenberg, J. S. (1985). Health and wellness: A conceptual differentiation. *Journal of School Health, 55*(10), 403-406.

Hackman, H. W. (2005). Five essential components for social justice education. *Equity & Excellence in Education, 38*(2), 103-109.

Harbour, C. P., & Ebie, G. (2011). Deweyan democratic learning communities and student marginalization. *New Directions for Community Colleges, 2011*(155), 5-14.

Howes, C., & Matheson, C. C. (1992). Sequences in the development of competent play with peers: Social and social pretend play. *Developmental Psychology, 28*(5), 961.

Jay, J. K., & Johnson, K. L. (2002). Capturing complexity: A typology of reflective practice for teacher education. *Teaching and teacher education, 18*(1), 73-85.

Jog, M. S., Kubota, Y., Connolly, C. I., Hillegaart, V., & Graybiel, A. M. (1999). Building neural representations of habits. *Science, 286*(5445), 1745-1749.

Kessen, W. (1979). The American child and other cultural inventions. *American Psychologist, 34*(10), 815.

Lambert, L. (2003). Leadership redefined: An evocative context for teacher leadership. *School leadership & management, 23*(4), 421-430.

Lee, K. H. (2005). The relationship between creative thinking ability and creative personality of preschoolers. *International Education Journal, 6*(2), 194-199.

Loughran, J. J. (2002). Effective reflective practice: In search of meaning in learning about teaching. *Journal of teacher education, 53*(1), 33-43.

Louis, K. S., Leithwood, K., Wahlstrom, K. L., Anderson, S. E., Michlin, M., & Mascall, B. (2010). Learning from leadership: Investigating the links to improved student learning.

Center for Applied Research and Educational Improvement/University of Minnesota and Ontario Institute for Studies in Education/University of Toronto, 42, 50.

Myers, J. E., Sweeney, T. J., & Witmer, J. M. (2000). The wheel of wellness counseling for wellness: A holistic model for treatment planning. *Journal of Counseling & Development, 78*(3), 251-266.

Pellegrini, A. D., & Smith, P. K. (1998). Physical activity play: The nature and function of a neglected aspect of play. *Child Development, 69*(3), 577-598.

Quintana, S. M., Aboud, F. E., Chao, R. K., Contreras-Grau, J., Cross, W. E., Hudley, C., ... & Vietze, D. L. (2006). Race, ethnicity, and culture in child development: Contemporary research and future directions. *Child Development, 77*(5), 1129-1141.

Riehle, C. F., & Weiner, S. A. (2013). High-impact educational practices: An exploration of the role of information literacy. *College & Undergraduate Libraries, 20*(2), 127-143.

Scholar.(2018). Retrieved March 8, 2018, from www.merriam-webster.com/dictionary/scholar

Schwartz, B. (2009). *The paradox of choice. Why more is less: Why the culture of abundance robs us of satisfaction.* New York, NY: Harper Collins

Schwartz, S. H. (1994). Are there universal aspects in the structure and contents of human values? *Journal of Social Issues, 50*(4), 19-45.

Seyranian, V., & Bligh, M. C. (2008). Presidential charismatic leadership: Exploring the rhetoric of social change. *Leadership Quarterly, 19*(1), 54-76.

Sleeter, C. E. (2012). Confronting the marginalization of culturally responsive pedagogy. *Urban Education, 47*(3), 562-584.

Smearsoll, G. (2017). Students as environmental educators. *Science Teacher, 84*(4), 51.

Smuts, J.C. (1926). *Holism and evolution.* New York, NY: Macmillan.

Smylie, M. A., & Denny, J. W. (1990). Teacher leadership: Tensions and ambiguities in organizational perspective. *Educational administration quarterly*, *26*(3), 235-259.

Sparks-Langer, G. M., & Colton, A. B. (1991). Synthesis of research on teachers' reflective thinking. *Educational Leadership, 48*(6), 37-44.

Taie, S., & Goldring, R. (2017). Characteristics of public elementary and secondary school teachers in the United States: Results from the 2015-16 National Teacher and Principal Survey. First Look (NCES 2017-072). U.S. Department of Education. Washington, DC: National Center for Education Statistics. Retrieved April 25, 2018 from http://nces.ed.gov/pubsearch/pubsinfo.asp:pubid=2017072

Villegas, A. M. (1988). School failure and cultural mismatch: Another view. *Urban Review, 20*(4), 253-265.

Walkington, J. (2005). Becoming a teacher: Encouraging development of teacher identity through reflective practice. *Asia-Pacific Journal of teacher education*, *33*(1), 53-64.

Wood, W., & Neal, D. T. (2007). A new look at habits and the habit-goal interface. *Psychological Review, 114*(4), 843.

York-Barr, J., & Duke, K. (2004). What do we know about teacher leadership? Findings from two decades of scholarship. *Review of educational research*, *74*(3), 255-316.

www.ingramcontent.com/pod-product-compliance
Lightning Source LLC
Chambersburg PA
CBHW080440110426
42743CB00016B/3228